Kaballah and the Ascension

DAVID K. MILLER

Other Publications by
David K. Miller

Teachings from the Sacred Triangle

New Spiritual Technology for the Fifth-Dimensional Earth

Connecting with the Arcturians

Raising the Spiritual Light Quotient

Kaballah

and the Ascension

channeled by DAVID K. MILLER

Light Technology
PUBLISHING

Cover art: *Millennium Tree (Tree of Peace)*, by Josephine Wall,
www.JosephineWall.com

*   *   *

ISBN-10: 1-891824-82-1
ISBN-13: 978-1-891824-82-1

Published and printed in the United States of America by:

PO Box 3540
Flagstaff, AZ 86003
800-450-0985
www.lighttechnology.com

TABLE OF CONTENTS

PREFACE

C hanneling is both a modern and a historical phenomenon and is found in all times and across all cultures. Throughout history, channeling has come to us in various forms, including medium-ship, shamanism, fortunetelling, visionaries, and oracles. There is also a long history of channeling in *Kaballah*, the major branch of Jewish mysticism. I have been a student of *Kaballah* for more than twenty-five years; I was raised as a Jew and have always been fascinated by the Hebrew language and have obtained a moderate knowledge of biblical Hebrew. This includes knowledge of the alphabet and Hebrew prayers, which are key ingredients in Kaballistic work.

Key phrases of a major Hebrew prayer are now being used by students of the Keys of Enoch for obtaining higher levels of consciousness. The sacred words "Holy, Holy, Holy [is] the Lord of Hosts" (*Kadosh, Kadosh, Kadosh Adonai Tzevaoth*) are power words—words that can raise one's level of consciousness. I was excited to learn that the Arcturians and Pleiadians also use the Hebrew name for God, *Adonai*, when referring to the Creator. Many Hebrew phrases have galactic origins, especially such power phrases.

THE HIGHER SELF

I have studied psychology for many years and have also been interested in altered states of consciousness, spirituality, and trance states. As a psychotherapist, I studied and observed the trance state—referred to in psychotherapy as the hypnotic state and trance induction. I know that this state can be a powerful tool for healing psychological and spiritual problems.

In 1987, my wife Gudrun and I moved to Arizona. I was fascinated by the spiritual opportunities in Sedona, Arizona, and I began attending lectures and channeling sessions. Many people were engaged in the process, which fascinated me. At the same time, I became aware that many of the ancient Kaballistic rabbis had also engaged in channeling! They referred to the process of trance mediumship as automatic speaking. It was a common practice in fifth-century Palestine for a Kaballistic student to lay his body over the grave of an ancient master and hope that information would be received from him.

Other famous rabbis, such as Joseph Karo, secretly practiced channeling and even wrote several channeled books. Some of these rabbis believed that they could channel the *Shekhinah*, or the feminine spirit of the Lord. Generally, their channeling was kept a secret. For example, Karo was an expert in Jewish law and well-respected for his work, the *Shulhan Aruch*, or the Set Table, which is a legalistic description of Jewish law in the fifth century. Most Jewish people, as well as the general population, do not know of his concurrent channeling practice.

The Seth materials and Lazarus have influenced me as well as channelings through Norma Milanovich and Barbara Marciniak (authors of *We, the Arcturians* and *Bringers of the Dawn*, respectively). The *Kaballah* allows for the concept of higher consciousness, or higher self, as a conduit for accessing higher realms. It is the higher self, or *Neshamah*, that is used in channeling to access higher light. Kaballists also believe in reincarnation. Although the *Kaballah* does not address the subject of extra-planetary beings, it does talk about soul families and deceased spirits of masters coming back to help students. They even allow for the concept of walk-ins, because they believe that one can be possessed by another spirit—referred to as *dybbuk* for bad spirits or *ibburs* for good spirits.

OTHER BEINGS WANT TO COMMUNICATE WITH US

I first spontaneously started channeling while on a camping trip at Sublime Point at the North Rim of the Grand Canyon in 1991. The energy at that point in the canyon was incredible. I became activated and began relating information to my wife about her past lives and relationships. During and after the experience, I had an incredible feeling of well-being. I felt excited and eager to continue. At the time I began my channeling, I had no idea that I would be bringing through many different guides, and since 1991 I have continued to channel on a regular basis. Because I had taped the channeled sessions, writing them down became the next logical step. It was my hope that I would eventually use the material in a book.

I think it is important to address the issue of whether channeling is real or the channel is engaged in a psychotic fugue state. Psychosis implies a gross impairment in one's ability to perceive normal reality. Our normal waking consciousness is one type of reality. The dream world is an example of another altered state in which telepathic reception of messages occurs. Thus, it is my belief that the channel can "sanely enter other realms," bringing down valuable and new energy from the outer realms. The fact that ancient rabbis engaged in channeling adds credence to the process. In fact, a substantial argument can be made that the earlier prophets and saints were also channels of light and energy from the higher realms. Notable channels of the twentieth century include: Edgar Cayce, Alice Bailey, Ruth Montgomery, and Arthur Ford.

Accepting channeling means that one has to put aside conventional beliefs. One must believe that our consciousness can go into other dimensions, that there are other-dimensional beings outside of our normal range of consciousness that wish to communicate with us, that there is reincarnation and life after death, and that those beings are interested in communicating with us. Finally, one must believe that there might be other beings in the universe— extraterrestrials, if you will—who also want to communicate with us.

In my channeling, I seek to receive information from all higher beings—beings that are well respected. Thus, if one hears comments from an archangel, then certainly one feels honored and open to the messages. Are we more likely to respect and listen to messages coming from another dimension? I think that, generally, people who are open to channeling do seem to respect a message from a higher being. However, we must always maintain discernment in any messages we receive.

I am intrigued by the long history of channeling in Western culture and in *Kaballah*. I believe that there is now a necessity for entering the higher realms with our consciousness. It is important to do so because of the impending changes on the planet. New healing energy and insights can be brought down to assist us in the coming Earth changes.

THE IMPORTANCE OF CHANNELING

The channeling sessions in this book were held in the Prescott, Arizona area. I have found the experience of channeling and writing these lectures stimulating and energizing. My wife Gudrun has provided great assistance in helping to transcribe the sessions. She has also provided positive emotional support and encouragement for the process.

I think it is time that modern psychology and religion consider the channeling phenomenon seriously. After all, many famous mystics were powerful and influential users of altered states of consciousness. I myself do not represent any school of mysticism. Rather, I consider myself a student of spiritual and mystical consciousness interested in obtaining and maintaining higher levels of being.

I currently reside with my wife Gudrun in Prescott, Arizona. The focus of my channeling includes ascension and integrating mysticism with soul development.

CHAPTER 1

KABALLAH AND
SOUL DEVELOPMENT

Nabur[1]

We are delighted to come here to talk about the different levels of soul development. We want to talk about the higher self, the middle self, and the lower self. We also want to explain to you a little bit about the channeling experience. You know that the channeling experience is something that you are all able to do. It is not something that is far out; it is a part of your path. It is something that each of you can use to tune in to your teachers. This is especially useful now, for your guides and teachers have specific information that will help you. We are with you, and this is a very exciting time in terms of the tremendous changes that are going on. It is important that you be able to access information that is peculiar to the level of your soul.

Each of you belongs to a specific soul group. Many of you are already aware of some of your brothers and sisters on the soul level. Those in your soul group are especially able to give you information that will help you to resonate with them. I want to emphasize the word "resonate." We are trying to help you to learn to resonate with the particular frequency that belongs to your soul. There are also other souls who can resonate at your particular frequency and who will help you to raise your consciousness.

We are talking about the *Kaballah* and the particular frequencies of the Hebrew language that are useful in tuning in to your soul vibrations. Hebrew is a special galactic language that was brought to Earth many centuries ago. It has certain sounds that resonate with the galactic core and help to bring in the Creator energy. This is extremely important. Many of the sounds themselves, even if you do not know what their meanings are, can take you into a higher state of consciousness. When you are in a higher state of consciousness, you can access your higher self. This is what you are about. This is one of the reasons you are incarnating now—so that you can access your higher self and tune in to the Creator.

As a warm-up, we are going to use the Hebrew word *Atah* to help you raise your vibrations. We are asking you to repeat this word: *"Atah . . . Atah . . . Atah."*[2]

When you say the word, feel the energy rising from the bottom of your spine up to the top. Sense a circle of energy around your auric field. As you say the word *Atah*, it vibrates your auric field, and your aura will begin to expand. When it expands, it is opening, allowing you to receive higher-level information. This is useful when you are trying to access higher energy fields.

THE ANIMAL SELF

There are three levels of self. You have the lower self, which some call the animal self. That sounds as if you are equal to the animal, which is in one sense true—you are an animal in your day-to-day functioning, and your survival skills are governed by this aspect. Your lower self has a unique ability, though: It can blend with your middle self. Unless your lower self is able to key into this energy, you cannot go into the middle self.

Many people on the planet are struggling to get their physical health in balance. There is a misconception that you must be in perfect physical health in order to resonate with the higher energy. Now, of course it is desirable to be in perfect physical health, but realistically, there are not many people who are going to have perfect physical harmony at this time. This is partly due to the fact that Earth is now polluted and that there are many chemicals affecting your body. It is also partly due to the ultraviolet radiation affecting your auric field. Finally, it is simply rare to be 100 percent in harmony. So go with the best level you can attain.

Now, even if you are disabled or even if you have an illness such as cancer, you can still resonate at a very high level. So don't think that if you are not totally healthy physically or if you have a major illness, you cannot reach the highest level. Of course you can! In fact, sometimes it is because of an illness that you can be driven to go on to a high energy level. On the other hand, you might be in perfect physical health—and have your animal self in perfect harmony—yet still be unable to reach the higher levels. When you go into the middle level and the higher levels, then you begin to access the highest energy fields and can bring in the soul energy, which will help you learn more about yourself. You will be able to access energy that will expand your lightbody.

Now, what do I mean by lightbody? The lightbody is that part of your higher self that will come down and merge with your lower self. In effect, this is the message of *Kaballah*: You can receive yourself. I am not saying that you must be selfish or narcissistic. What I am saying is that you have a higher lightbody that is able to coordinate and merge with your lower self on this plane. When you can do this, you have access to untold secrets of the universe, you have access to fantastic energies, and you can transcend your physical ego and go into higher energy states.

When we talk about channeling, when we work with the channel, or when we help others to channel, what we are doing is helping you, the seeker, to access your higher self. When you are in that state, you can access the energy fields of other entities that are in the same resonance. And now I am going to go back to the term "resonance." In accessing higher energy states, you are preparing your physical body so that you can resonate with your higher self. Only then can your higher self resonate with the other energies. When you are bringing down higher energy, that energy is only as powerful as the connection you can make. Your body, physical presence, and mind become the tools. Your mind, voice, and speech are like a computer for the energy that is coming through. If there is a glitch in the computer or if there are certain words that the computer does not have in its vocabulary, then those words cannot be brought forth.

CHANNELING PAST MASTERS AND TEACHERS

I want to speak about the past masters and the *Kaballah*. One of the important aspects of *Kaballah* study focuses on channeling past masters and teachers. Many Kaballists were interested in working with the past masters, whom they could channel. Channeling was a very common experience in the ancient days. Even as recently as a century or two ago, many were still actively engaged in channeling and were using channeling predominantly as a means of obtaining specific information.

Channeling does need to have some safeguards. If you are channeling, you need to have a sense that you are bringing down higher energy. There must be a sense of protection from any negative entities who might enter. Also, you must realize that you are doing the channeling for a specific purpose: to expand the light energy and the energy fields of yourself and of those who are listening. It is extremely important that you keep those ideas in mind.

We want to work more with sounds, because as much as we can give you words, sound vibrations are even more powerful in opening up your mind. Now we are going to work with the sound of *Hu*.[3] I would like you to put your hand over your third eye[4] and then vibrate your third-eye chakra as you say, "*Hu . . . Hu . . . Huuu . . . Huuuu . . .*" Sit with your energy now. We are working to open up your energy field, in particular the third eye, because when it is open, you will be able to receive more information. When one energy field opens, then the other ones also want to be open, although sometimes it is more difficult to open up the second one.

We want to go to the crown chakra[5] now. The crown chakra can be opened up with the Hebrew word for our father—*Adonai*, or Lord. Say: "*Adonai . . . Adonai . . . Adonai . . .*"

An opening has now occurred on the planet through which you are able to get to the highest energy fields if you have the proper concentration and use the proper sounds. It does not take years and years of study or practice. The time frame for being on Earth is limited. There are about to be major shifts of energy and major upheavals. If you are able to access your highest energy—if you are able to access the Creator energy and open up to receive information from your highest self—then it is important that you do so. It is important for you and for the planet. You want to get yourself into the best possible spiritual shape.

Many of you already are going through major physical problems and imbalances. This is going to continue as long as the energy field around the planet is in so much fluctuation that it is very difficult to maintain a balance.

THE SPLENDOR OF THE LIGHT

Now let us talk about being able to get in touch with the higher self, which in the *Kaballah* is called the *neshamah*.[6] With the *neshamah*, you are able to access your psychic abilities to the highest level. You are able to look into the future. You are able to look into the past. You are able to look into the pasts and futures of others. Now this sounds like an extraordinary ability, but it is not. It is a gift. It is something that you all are able to do. You have the genetic code for it, you have the mental structure, you have the ability to align your mental bodies, and you have the historical precedent. The only thing blocking you is your belief that it is out of your range. It is not. Each of you can look at other people and even look into yourselves and experience past lives.

Many people are surprised to learn that the *Kaballah* and the *Zohar*[7] have their origins in the galactic energy. You are not alone in the universe. Much of the information that has reached this planet has been coming from other sources. There is a universal language and there are galactic sounds, many of which are in Hebrew. For example, the term *Zohar* refers to the light, or the splendor of the light.

So much of what we are about as spiritual beings has to do with light. There are many different ramifications of light. There are many different light rays, and there is so much light available. People talk about the darkness that is now on the Earth plane—the hatred, the densities, the pollution, and so forth. Yet light can penetrate even darkness. You are now able to bring in more of your own light. The key is to bring in the light from your lightbody and from your highest self.

I wish to talk now about the opening of the heart. The path of the light, the path that ascends up the ladder, is based in your heart chakra.[8] The heart chakra is the center of the Tree of Life. It is there that you can access all energies that are available, including energies of the highest form. By accessing the heart sphere, you can receive a sliver, a spark, of all the other spheres.

It is a mistake to believe that you can do this work without opening up your heart. The heart is the key to the soul. Your heart energy and your ability to love yourself and others are vitally important. The highest form of love is the love of the Creator energy, our Father/Mother. When you are able to tap into that love, you will have the love that will help you accept yourself and love yourself.

UNDERSTANDING WITH THE HEART ENERGY

The difficulty in loving the Creator is that you often get lost trying to understand the Creator with your mind. This is a wonderful intellectual exercise, a wonderful philosophical exercise. It has produced volumes and volumes of beautiful writings. But in the true *Kaballah* and on the true path of mysticism, humans understand the love of the Creator with heart energy. When that is accomplished, you are not able to explain it; you are not able to describe it.

I want you to take a moment to experience the love of the Creator, *Adonai,* in your heart and see what it feels like. You might find that the first step in the process is to receive the love of the Creator personally. This is extremely powerful if you are able to open up your heart chakra to that love. It will fill you.

Now I want you to sense the love of the Creator. If you can, I would like you to feel the burst of light that began creation. That burst of light is the substance of your soul. You are on a path to realize your place in creation, and the path of light will help you to align with your soul families. One of the key beliefs of *Kaballah* is that you are part of soul families, and some of your soul families are in the other dimensions. They are eagerly awaiting your return.

Is "atah" a word or just a sound?

Atah is the Hebrew word for "you," and with this word, we are referring to the Creator. We are speaking of the Creator as "You." You can use many forms and vibrations to call forth the Creator energy. Basically, you are announcing that you are ready to vibrate your aura on the Creator's energy wavelength. You can use any of the many names of God to do that.

What can we do to expand into the Creator energy?

Each of you resonates with a particular name of God, with particular sounds that work for you better than others do. You will have to experiment to see which is the best one. The energy of *atah* is one of the basic sounds, and you can practice it in your meditations. Many of you are aware of the mantra meditations of the yogis in which they say Om, for example. The sound of *atah* is just as powerful, and it will awaken in you the vibratory fields much more quickly. We suggest you choose the sound you feel most resonant with and use that. Experiment with saying it softly and saying it loudly. Say it mentally or visualize it on a screen. Obviously, you will want to be in a meditative state. Some of you can use it when you feel you are in danger. You might be driving down the street and think a car is going to hit you. Say *atah,* and suddenly your energy field will begin to expand and white light will extend outward. You then have an energy shield that is protecting you.

There are many different ways of using the sounds, but we find that it is important that the sound be vocalized, even if you vocalize it to yourself very softly. There must be an actual expression of the sound.[9] This is one of the beauties of the Hebrew language. The sounds themselves are on a special vibratory wavelength that resonates with a special energy field that will help to expand your energy field.

Notes:

1. Nabur is a Kaballistic rabbi and teacher of the channel in a former lifetime.
2. *Atah*: the Hebrew word for "you." In the *Amidah*, a famous prayer in the Jewish service, the first opening blessing is called Fathers. It begins: "Blessed are You, O Lord . . ."
3. *Hu*: the Hebrew word for "he." In prayers, it can refer to the Creator.
4. Third eye: the Ajna chakra, located centrally on the forehead. This chakra reflects the polarity of Binah-Chokmah, the second and third Sephiroth on the Tree of Life.
5. Crown chakra: the Sahasrara chakra, located about the crown fontanelle on the skull. This chakra reflects the unity of tKether, the first Sephirah on the Tree of Life.
6. Neshamah: the highest of the three parts of the soul. Literally "breath" or "spirit," it is the intuitive power that connects humankind with the Creator.
7. *Zohar: The Book of Splendor*, a thirteenth-century Spanish mystic's guide to Kaballism.
8. Heart chakra: the Anahata chakra, located along the central meridian, close to the heart. Reflects the equilibrium of Tiphareth, the sixth Sephirah of the Tree of Life.
9. See Appendix A for a brief discussion on the Romanization and pronunciation of Hebrew words found in the text.

CHAPTER 2

PATH WORK

Sananda[1]

I t is helpful to prepare yourselves by going into trances. Doing so helps you to open yourselves up to receive information. You are working diligently on your paths, and many of you are curious about them, wondering whether you are on the right path and how to continue to develop and improve your path work. The paths you are maintaining are like doorways into different spiritual realms. Each path you walk on has a particular benefit and a particular experience for you that will ultimately enhance your soul's development.

Let us look at the question of how beneficial the pain that people experience in this incarnation can be. You must understand that you are choosing paths based on how they enhance your soul development, not necessarily based on how painful it might be. Some will have pain, yet you cannot measure the success of your path by the amount of pain you have; rather, you can measure the success of your path by whether or not it has been enhancing your particular soul level. That is really the true test of a path.

Some of you have been on paths that have allowed you to be extremely materially successful. Yet even though things have come very easily for you financially, you might not have enhanced yourself. Some of you are on soul paths filled with outward material ease so that you have the opportunity to develop free will to study or perhaps branch out in new directions. The opportunity in these cases is left up to you to develop. You then have the ability to fulfill your soul purposes and broaden your paths. Many of you now have the opportunity to finish a broadening of your soul's development.

There are many people around you involved in spiritual work, but you must understand that there are many souls on the planet who have no sense of spiritual work at all and who have no spiritual sensitivities. This is the general condition on the planet. Even if you involve yourself in religious studies, you do not necessarily understand your soul path, and understanding your soul path is the final piece you must integrate to complete your mission.

Volumes can be written about the soul, about what it means to have a soul, and what it means to lose contact with it. Losing your soul contact is a worse condition than having a painful life filled with poverty. Evaluate a life not according to whether there is pain but according to whether there is any meaningful soul contact, despite the painful lessons. It could be that particular lessons have come through painfully because of misguided thought processes that can now be changed.

The Role of Divine Guidance

Every path is different. Each of you is following your path to the best of your abilities. However, you are not taking as much time as you could to check in and receive messages. It is extremely important to do this. One of the more beautiful aspects of the *Kaballah* and the Tarot is that they offer charts of paths that show different levels. They can be good study tools, providing a visual display of the stages you follow through incarnations.

Path work involves understanding that materialism is an illusion. Each of you will approach materialism from a different level. Some of you will attempt to understand it as an illusion and might decide not to have material possessions. Some will have possessions but simply decide they are not important. Others will have material possessions and be influenced by them to the point that you lose your spiritual contact. All aspects of materialism are to be evaluated on the basis of whether or not they hinder your spiritual contact. If you are without material possessions but have lost your soul contact, then you are not really achieving anything. If you have material possessions and have great soul contact, then you are not hindered by the possessions. You can enjoy the material things and continue to make progress.

Basic path work includes an understanding of life and death. Some of you are not able to go beyond a basic understanding of the life-and-death cycle. Many of you still do not appreciate that it is a miracle to exist here, especially when you consider the improbability of a life form being in a particular place on a particular planet in a specific star system.

It is truly a miracle that your personal life has evolved to the point at which you can remain healthy given the incalculable intervening factors that occur in an incarnation. Knowing this should give you a sense that life would not be possible without divine guidance and intervention. There have been many times in your life when you could have died or become ill with a major disease. It is important to understand and accept that divine guidance plays a role in your life. At the same time, there can exist a sense of separation, an anxiety that there is no further life. When you lose your sense of divine guidance, it can lead to the fear that after this incarnation, you will be left without existence.

It is important to become aware of what you can do—what is unique about your abilities and how you can best be of service. This level of awareness develops when you focus on your mission of service, including service to yourself. Make no mistake: Serving yourself is a valuable mission. Every soul who incarnates must go through certain developmental stages and achieve a specific level in order to ascend. Although there are many people to help, do not underestimate the need to serve yourself, because when you do so, you will be fostering your own soul's development. This is not selfish; it is part of the path. If it were not important to serve yourself, why would other guides and entities bother to serve you? This is a very important question to ask yourself. You are important! If you do not think you are important, then why would the masters bother to spend time with you?

When you are grappling with that situation of service, understand that you can also be of service to other people in various ways. It could be at high levels such as giving instructions and teaching, or it could be simply helping in material or physical ways. What is important is that service and path work give you a sense of growth and expansion.

SUGGESTIONS FOR PATH WORK

You said earlier that we need to keep checking in about our paths, and you suggested we use the Kaballah and the Tarot. Should we use them in traditional ways?

What I am saying is that the *Kaballah* and the Tarot are representations of path work. I am not saying that they are the final answer. They are some of the models that are available to you; there might be other models. You can use them as a springboard for understanding path work.

Are there other ways of discerning whether or not you are on the correct path?

There is not a single tool that can discern whether you are on the correct path. There are many tools to make you *aware* of paths. Certain Native American peoples, for example, arrive at a sense of their paths by using meditations, vision quests, sweats, and walks. They use universal archetypal stages of soul development. Thus you can see that a broader perspective is helpful—one that encompasses an understanding of more than just the present incarnation. Allow yourself to receive more information about your path work from personal guides in meditations.

Notes:

1. Sananda is the one who is known to us as Master Jesus. Joshua ben Miriam—Jesus, son of Mary—is considered the greatest Kaballist of all time. He has chosen a new name—Sananda—to represent an evolved and galactic picture of who he is now. "My task on Earth has been to serve as a vehicle for that Christ consciousness which has anchored love into the Earth . . ." Dorothy Roeder, *Reach for Us* (Sedona, AZ: Light Technology Publishing, 1995), 93.

CHAPTER 3

SOUL PSYCHOLOGY

Vywamus

e would like to talk about soul psychology. As much as we talk about the higher energy levels and about the light, you still come back to many of the psychological problems that you have on the lower and middle soul levels. These are the problems you wrestle with from day to day, and problems that elude you or that you don't want to recognize in yourself usually have spiritual significance.

In previous lifetimes, many of you have gone to higher energy states only to tumble down because you hadn't worked out these "minor" problems. At that time you called them little blocks, and you didn't really think they were important. Yet you soon found yourselves in a rather embarrassing position or in a position in which there seemed to be no way out. Then you lost your spiritual power and the ability to vibrate on higher energy waves. This is why it is so important to work out these problems now. Don't think that simply because it is a problem of the lower soul or the lower personality, it is not crucial. Don't think that the middle personality isn't important. These problems you are having—some of which are psychological problems—are very important.

YOUR RESISTANCE TO SPIRITUAL KNOWLEDGE

Now the question comes up: "Why do these problems occur to people? Why are you having these life problems? What is the significance of them?" Some might say that you asked for the problem in order to teach yourself a lesson. Wasn't that nice, to offer yourself such a difficult lesson? Well, that is an interesting way to look at it, but when you are in the middle of the lesson, then it seems more difficult. You wish that you could terminate the lesson immediately. In truth, you can actually drop the lesson if you move and expand your consciousness. Then you can take the next growth step. When you expand your consciousness and recognize the necessary personal lesson, then the problem and its significance will not be dominating your lives. When you recognize the personal lesson, then the problem you are struggling with will take its proper perspective.

It is your reaction to the problem that is as important as the problem itself. Think about the number-one problem in your life today. Right now, think of your reaction to it. Can you report what your reaction is to the problem? You have had a chance to learn a great spiritual truth. You could be wiser and spiritually alive if you learned to solve the problem. What is your reaction? Are you open to solving this?

Many may be reluctant. It is true that you want to gain spiritual knowledge; you want access to higher knowledge and to higher energies. Yet when it comes down to working on your personal problems, there is resistance. Why? The reason for this is that you are reluctant to go through a difficult experience. It is that reaction that is creating the resistance. On this plane, you know a lot about resistance. Resistance is self-generating. Resistance is like a snowball coming down a mountain, getting larger and larger. Many of your psychologists have developed a great idea that has spiritual significance: In order to help people to grow psychologically, you have to help them deal with resistance. What a beautiful thought!

Most of you did not want to come into this incarnation. You wanted to stay where you were. It was like being in the mother's womb, and then you got kicked out! Who wants to leave that comfortable place? You know that if you are too comfortable, then you don't grow, but no one wants to leave his or her comfortableness. Yet there is no guarantee that the comfort will continue forever. I have great respect and admiration for your courage in coming back and dealing with this incarnation in order to continue struggling with your soul problems.

THE CONFLICT OF BELIEF

I will also say that there is a general law you can observe: The greater the reaction, the more important this problem is on your spiritual path. What a great indicator you have! I would guess that the problems you have are problems you don't want. Even though you know they have the potential to give you great spiritual gifts and great path openings, you still might not feel that it is worth the struggle you are going through.

This brings you back to the basic principle of belief systems and your mental body: the source of much of your conflict. You need to put yourself at peace with these problems. You can change them by working with your belief systems. You can also open yourself up to what it is you need to learn. I am going to ask each of you to tell me what the lesson is that you need to learn from your personal problems. Affirm:

> *I am not attached to the outcome.*
> *I know that I am not in control.*
> *I accept the truth of my body.*
> *I let go and trust.*
> *I know I will be guided to where I need to go with it.*
> *I have faith in myself.*

What beautiful lessons! If I told you that I had a group of people who were working on these lessons, wouldn't you be impressed? Wouldn't you think that they were highly evolved? [Laughs.] So why aren't you impressed with yourselves? These are core soul issues that you are working on. You are right in there with the meat and potatoes of your spiritual growth.

Your resistance is also easier to overcome when you are able to share it in a group. When you are able to gain a different perspective on yourself and the problem, then you will be pleased. You will be able to accelerate the problem to a quicker conclusion. Being stuck simply means that there is no movement.

There are only two ways to get out of a problem: You can change, or the people who are creating the problem can change. You have control over yourself, over how you change and how you are interpreting the events. You have minor control over the other part. When you change, the energies interacting between the problem and you become different. How many of you believe that you can affect the outcome by your whole attitude, your perspective and how you think about the problem? Your thoughts can create possible outcomes. How many of you focus on negative outcomes? Don't be afraid to admit it. We won't hold it against you.

THE MIRACLE OF LESSONS LEARNED

If I told you that focusing on negative outcomes increases the possibility that they will come true, would you still hold that focus? There is a way to work around the problem of negative thinking. You have to get a soul perspective on why you are in the situation and what the lesson is. It would be a good idea to write down the lesson and post it on the wall so that you can look at it every day. Remind yourself of that lesson; you are in control of your reaction to the problem. Beliefs are that powerful.

Beliefs are so powerful that they could even affect the outcome. It is true that you are not in control of everything, but you are still a player in this, and you can have an effect on the outcome through your attitude. You know that people dying of cancer have miraculous remissions. This occurs because they have changed their perspectives. You have come into this incarnation to work on these problems, and when you are able to state the lesson, then you are at least 50 percent of the way through the process.

At this point you might ask, "What do I need to do in order to learn the lesson finally?" The last word is so important: "finally." You probably had this problem in another lifetime, but you didn't learn it. Now you have another chance to do it. Let's finally do it. If you cannot answer the question of what you finally need to do, then meditate on it. Your soul involvement is such that you want to solve this problem as soon as possible, and it is possible to be done with it once you are able to learn the lesson. The whole problem might not go away, but you could find some remarkable relief. The energy field around the problem will lessen, and you will be very surprised at the amount of negative energy that will stop coming your way. Then you will have more energy to focus on spiritual work.

CHAPTER 4

THE ETHERIC REALM

Sananda

W e speak with you now about the etheric realm. This realm can be considered the interface between your third dimension and the fifth dimension. It is in this realm that it is easier for us to make contact with you. Many of you still have resistance to entering the higher realms, but you can still experience parts of the etheric realm in your sleep and through dreams. That is only one aspect of the etheric realm, however, and sometimes even that aspect of your dream experience is filled with densities from the third dimension.

The etheric realm is the realm that is vibrating at the next higher frequency compared to the frequency you are now familiar with in the third dimension. When you begin to sense the higher realm, you begin to sense a vibrational experience in yourself and in others. You begin to see energy fields around others. You begin to sense or actually see the auras around them.

In yourself, you begin to sense very directly that you are more than just this dense substance that you call yourself or that you call your body. You are, in fact, vibrating. Your energy field and energy existence are very broad. They extend far beyond the physical presence you normally observe in yourself or in others. Sensing this field is the beginning of awareness of the etheric realm. Some of you are initially confused and scared when you see the waviness of the etheric dimension. You might think that you are going crazy or that you are losing your mind. You might fear that you will not be able to return to the normal state of consciousness that you now share on the third dimension.

You know that this "normal" state of consciousness is an agreed-upon level that you have been brought up to experience. Some of you understand that you can experience higher states naturally by unlearning old patterns. The biggest pattern you need to unlearn focuses on thinking. Your ability to perceive the higher dimension and etheric realm is directly proportional to what you believe and think you can experience and see. When you believe that you can experience and see these realms, then you will begin to open up to them.

It is similar to the experience many of you are struggling with as you are learning to channel; it is a letting go. It is not something that I can tell you to practice or do, although there is some direction that can be offered. The final direction is simply that you will be able to let go with the understanding that you are letting go to gain an awareness and understanding of the etheric realm.

THE STATE OF EXPANSION

The beginning levels of the etheric realm are the energy fields—the perception and sensing of the energy fields. As you enter the etheric realm, you can go into deeper trances, achieve deeper levels of communication, and receive visitors and guides on deeper levels. In addition, you can do what some have described as astral traveling. You can move your consciousnesses and your etheric selves.

In the Hebrew language, we are aware that they use the word *Zelem*[1] for the etheric presence. *Zelem* has a ring to it that often can put you into a vibration that will help you resonate with that energy. *Zelem* represents the etheric body and the etheric self. When in contact with the *Zelem*, you can begin to travel and have contacts with other realms. When you can travel in those realms, you will begin to experience a personal transformation. You will be able to take the awareness of your third-dimensional physical selves and feel as if you are going through a door. You will pass through a realm that takes you to a higher reality. As you pass into that reality, you will find that you can take off a coat of density, a level of self that is not needed anymore; it is a level that is not useful when you decide to travel into the etheric realm.

I encourage you to practice going through this door. You will simply begin to vibrate and then, as you are sitting, you will begin to transform and vibrate with your energy field. Your energy field will expand. You must understand that in your normal density here, you are very contracted.

Your more natural state is a level of expansion that brings you beautifully into the etheric realm. You will experience tranquil vibration and waviness in that realm, and your experience of colors will be deeper. You will simply release your contractedness, which will help you to stop identifying with your denser selves in the third dimension.

Is the etheric realm where the plant devas exist?

Yes. They are one aspect of the etheric realm. They are not necessarily on the first level. When you bring your plants into Earth consciousness, you may use visualizations, especially to work with the etheric realm and to direct yourselves. The formats most often used in working with the etheric energy are visualization and sound. You may simply speak the name of the plant. You may visualize the plant, and it will guide you. The same level is also used when seeking your power animals.

Some have worried about the violence or negativity in the etheric. They are not truly in the etheric; instead, they are from the lower-density self that is at a level below the etheric. We prefer to call that the lower astral level. It is the level where you will find discarnate spirits and other negative energies that surround the planet. It is seething with aspects of the unconscious and preconscious levels. The etheric level is truly a protected level.

In meditations, I frequently experience mental traveling in which I actually meet masters and have experiences. Is that not astral traveling but part of the etheric realm?

You can astral travel into the etheric realm; astral traveling is part of the etheric awareness. So yes, to answer your question, you are experiencing things on the etheric. Some try to focus on going beyond the etheric, but if you go beyond the etheric and are stabilized, you could possibly leave this incarnation, which could be premature. That is why much of the contact that is now occurring with the guides and masters is occurring through the etheric. There is a sense that it is not the right time to bring you up to a higher level, for fear you would disincarnate before your time.

Each of you has a time that is allotted. It is interactive with your higher selves in terms of what is going on, so there could be minor modifications of when you leave. It is better to leave at an appropriate time and in an appropriate way for you. Some have had strange death experiences—such as someone very high in consciousness meeting a violent death, for example. Do not be concerned. It does not mean that their levels of consciousness were off, but simply that an accumulation of other karmic problems were resolved.

We are thinking specifically of the famous scientist and writer Itzhak Bentov here. He wrote a beautiful book called *Stalking the Wild Pendulum* and then died in a plane crash in 1979. He was doing wonderful work, gaining wonderful knowledge and understanding of the etheric realm. One of the problems with that, however, was that he went higher and higher. When you continue to go higher without a grounding base, then it becomes easier to disincarnate and you might look for the first opportunity to do so. This can be done, but there is much work to be done down here, and you will find that there is an advantage in your staying here a while longer.

OVERCOME YOUR APPREHENSION: HIGHER STATES UPLIFT YOU

I feel apprehensive about trying to go into this interface, because I feel I haven't done enough work on the third dimension to warrant it.

You must understand that accessing the fourth dimension will help with your third-dimensional work. It will give you another perspective. It will offer you an expansion. You might have the sense that you haven't done enough work to warrant entering the fourth dimension, but don't wait until that point when you feel: "Now I've done enough work." It is an interface, as you beautifully describe it, and working in the fourth dimension, despite the fears you have, will benefit your third-dimensional work by letting you be more expansive and by giving the soul's perspective on your problems.

You may look, for example, at the energy blocks you are experiencing in your third dimension. You might find that you can use energy work as a way of moving the blockages. You are psychologically and genetically constructed to experience and participate in the fourth dimension. It is part of your birthright and makeup, but you have been trained or educated not to do it. You have false beliefs about what the fourth dimension means, which is why you have some fear. You might believe that you are not worthy enough, that you will go crazy, or that you will not be able to stabilize the energy. These are fears based on belief systems.

I assure you that when you approach the dimensional transition gradually and with openness, you will be taken care of. Your guides will take care of you. You will not be overexposed or be overwhelmed by too much energy. I assure you that you will be helped. Think of it this way: When you go to a beautiful, high mountain, do you not feel uplifted? It is the same way when you go to a higher dimension from the third dimension. You will be able to experience from a beneficial perspective the feeling of being uplifted.

ACCESSING THE ETHERIC REALM

A lot of times when I go to Sedona, Arizona, I experience that waviness around vortex energies in a pronounced way.

It is a good idea to practice going to those places to begin to open yourself. You need to be recharged continually. Despite your commitment to this energy and this path, you are subject to the laws that are creating denser energies, and you can become more contracted. I encourage you to go to these places and work with the energy. It would be extremely helpful. It is good to combine your outdoor activities with the opportunity to access the different realms.

Part of the reason for the development of churches and religions has been to create vortices throughout the world so people could learn to experience the higher energy levels in various places. We are especially intrigued by the ability to do this in caves. I realize there is not easy access to caves everywhere, but there are some caves in your area [Northern Arizona] that are very powerful. The Native Americans in your area were very knowledgeable about using caves to access the etheric realm.

Another way to reach the etheric realm is through prayer. This is a very powerful way of preparation. When you are accessing the etheric realm, I encourage you to meditate and pray. Pray for divine guidance and for contact with the divine Creator energy. When you get in touch with the etheric realm, you are getting in touch with the Creator energy. You can consider contact with the etheric realm a way of deepening your connection with the Creator energy. When you frame it in this way, you have another protection around you that is really a protection of your mind.

You see, what you most need is protection from your own mind. When you can remove yourself from the mind, then you will find you can do wonderful things in the etheric realm. The mind needs to be taken care of. You cannot ignore it. The approach I recommend is to invoke the power of prayer. When you are asking for contact with the Creator energy, prayer can circumvent negative thoughts. The desire for divine contact is so strong that it cuts through many defenses and dense thought patterns that are contracting your energy fields. When you can think of the Creator energy, then you will begin to expand the contractions.

Think of the Creator energy in your own way. That is the way to begin your entry into the etheric. Even if you do not have a high opinion of yourself, you can still experience Creator energy. Allow whatever openings there are within you to embrace this light. It is especially this light from the Creator that fills the etheric realm and that draws you to it. You are like moths that seek the night light, but this light is the light of the Creator. When you are adhering to this light, you find that you do not need your fears. Your fears will simply fall away without effort.

Be open to the different levels of consciousness that you experience in sleep, such as being on the edge of sleep, falling to sleep, and coming out of sleep. Watch your sleeping tonight. You might be surprised at what will occur.

Notes:

1. From the *Zohar* and through Isaac Luria's teaching, an aspect of man is mentioned that is referred to in the *Kaballah* as the *Zelem*, the "image," based on Genesis 1:26: "Let us make man in our image, after our likeness" (King James Version). The *Zelem* is the principle of individuality with which every human being is endowed—the spiritual configuration, or essence, that is unique to him alone. One notion in this concept relates to man's ethereal garment, or ethereal (subtle) body, which serves as an intermediary between his material body and his soul. For more information, see Gershom Scholem, *Kabbalah* (Jerusalem: Keter Publishing House, 1974), 158.

CHAPTER 5

MOVING YOUR ELECTROMAGNETIC FIELD TO A HIGHER REALM

Sananda and Mary

I salute your work to integrate and be yourself. This is your mission and the measuring stick of this incarnation. It is not necessary to achieve A or B or C. What counts is that you be yourself. You are yourself when you bring the highest energy down to Earth to manifest health, prosperity and love. This includes love of yourself. It is required to manifest love for yourself.

You are an elaborate and complex being. Think of yourself as a magnificent electromagnetic, vibrating energy field that is eight to ten feet tall—a huge angelic presence connected to different realms. You are vibrating in another realm as I am speaking. This is your natural state. We are helping you to tap into your electromagnetic potential.

It is hard to comprehend that there exists another dimension that you can simultaneously interact with from Earth. Open up your crown chakra. Release any energy blocks from your solar plexus. Allow the energies to open you up. Moses came down from Mount Sinai with beams of light coming from his head and eyes. When you are in a highly electrical state, you do not want to leave it. You do not have to leave it! You can stay in it. Rise up in your dimensional presence. Move your electromagnetic field into the highest realm you can reach. Up! Up!

Being aware of who you are makes you feel magnificent. You are deeply connected to many beings on this planet and in other realms. In your manifestation here, you are not alone. I can assure you that you have at least fifteen or twenty guides that are overseeing this existence. They are helping you to contact other energies. They are trying to bring information down to you, hoping you will call on them. You are special in many ways. You really do have the ability to enter into the higher dimensions.

You have questions about the ascension[1]—when is it going to happen? We are moving there, I can assure you. There is a wonderful group consciousness and awareness on the planet. It is a force that is a presence. It is a factor that even three or four years ago was not here. This presence is multiplying at a nice rate.

It is true that many of you have opened to your dimensionalities. You can accept entering the other realms by means of an ascension path, and the energy is continuing to work through the planet in a healing way. It is appropriate for you to stay here a little longer so that you can anchor and spread the energy. As you are accomplishing that, you can learn to enter another realm.

Why don't we do this now? I will use some sounds and you can imagine yourself, as I am speaking, transforming into another dimension. [Makes sounds.] There are many sightings of Mother Mary. Sense her presence now in this room.

✳   ✳   ✳

Good evening. This is Mary. Each of you is valuable in this work of ascension and transformation. You are able to do this work through your own heart-opening and thinking. You can transform your energy presence by making yourself lighter and brighter.

Of course, there has been much unbalancing already, but you will know that you are closer to the energy transformation because of the number of calamities that continue in rapid sequence. We have told you over and over again: Try to not become attached to these events. Have faith in your ability to transform on all levels. Do not feel that you must resolve every difficulty. Remember that Sananda has promised and is fulfilling grace for those who are committing themselves. A period of grace was accelerated in 1994, and there were and will be other opportunities for even more magnificent work.

Many people on the planet are moving to the other side through the death process. We are busy helping them adjust. Some want to come back immediately because they understand the availability and the magnificence of work that can be done here. I inform you of the preciousness of your being alive and functioning now on Earth. It is desirable to be alive and functional on this planet. Keep your hearts open and connected to the galaxy.

ADDRESSING THE ASCENSION

Yes, it is true that the ascension and the transformation of Earth are a galactic operation. It is true that you have links throughout this galaxy. Some links are with other beings, such as the Pleiadians and the Arcturians. Some people even have links to the Andromeda Galaxy. It is fantastic. It means that you can call on other sources and bring their energy to Earth. We all know the planet needs much assistance and energy. Opening to multidimensionality is your mission. I cannot do it for you; I can only guide you.

There are energy interactions occurring continually, not only within the solar system but also outside of it. Thought patterns are coming from different sources to Earth. Earth is in the thoughts of many beings—more than you could count in third-dimensional thinking. Earth is playing a major role in shaping galactic events, and the outcome is critical to many beings. Allow as much energy as possible from these sources to come down and help to illuminate the true reality. Do not concentrate on the ego games and conflicts that you are seeing continually on the world stage. These are transitory. They have been played over and over again on the planet. Perhaps you have questions about the ascension?

When will we have world peace, and what will bring that about?

You are witnessing the formation of the one-world government. It is a dominating force that is going to direct this peace. There is a coalition of leaders who are seeking world control. This is based on events as they are unfolding today. Remember that all predictions are subject to change simply because of intervening variables and thoughts. For example, some of you can focus energy on an area such as California and postpone a dramatic catastrophe by sending love and light into that part of the planet.

Some will say, "But I thought the ascension was going to happen sooner." Remember, things have to unfold. People have to make choices. You remember free will, don't you?

Since hearing about the ascension in 1990, I have been doing lots of work on clearing and on accepting the soul. I find that I feel lighter and wonder if that is part of the ascension.

This is part of the ascension, which is a continual process. It will not be an abrupt shift as many of you have thought. It is true that there will be a sudden moment, but it will not be traumatic for those who are prepared and evolving. You make yourself lighter so that you can leave third-dimensional materialism and ego processes behind.

You are moving to a place where this will be easier. Remember your thoughts about the possibility of ascending two years ago? Look where you were then and think of today and what a difference there is in terms of the abruptness and the shifting. Becoming lighter will help you to continue work on the other side.

What year do you see for the ascension?

The ascension is occurring in stages; the final transformation is coming in steps. Now you are experiencing an overall period in which there are those dark and tumultuous forces that you might expect from a world cataclysm.

Is it possible that we might ascend first because we are raising our vibrations?

Yes. Some have already experimented and have been able to ascend from the planet. In terms of a group ascension, there has not yet been a mass ascension. I am talking about two or three million people. Originally it appeared that there was going to be only a small contingent. Now it appears that there will be a larger number. This will have a positive effect, not only on the people who ascend but also on the planet itself. It will be a demonstration of the power of Spirit over other forces. It will stimulate others to reconsider their values and embrace spirituality as a path. Some will be ready to look at their ways and change them.

Is the idea taking root now?

Very definitely. The process and transmission of the ascension energy has definitely solidified in many parts of the planet.

What of all the talk of war? Is that a diversion?

No, it is not a diversion. It is part of the ego process that is still occurring and is dominating the planet. It is a force and a threat at all times. It needs to be taken seriously.

Notes:

1. Ascension is a point of balance reached in physical existence that allows you to move to a new level of consciousness and a new plane of existence. It has been compared to what is called "the Rapture" in Christian theology.

CHAPTER 6

ON ANCHORING ENERGY

Sananda

W e will be working on anchoring both your energy and the gains you have made. It is important to stabilize your own foundation and have confidence that this foundation is in place. Thus you will not go backward. Anchoring is necessary in the process we are describing—the process of ascension. There are ups and downs in the ascension, but eventually you reach a plateau; you reach a sense of gain and progress. We call this the ability to anchor. By anchoring the energy, you are also able to stabilize your energy system.

If you look back on your development over the past six months, you will sense that you have already anchored energy. Think of those times when you were particularly high and resonating with the frequency that you felt was so etheric. Can you tune in and remember that?

Think of how nice it would be to establish a foundation or anchor so that you could return to that point at will. You could then establish a baseline. Think of your mountaineers who establish records climbing Mount Everest. Do they not have a base camp first? A base camp is very high on the mountain. It could be as high as 17,000 to 18,000 feet. Most people could not reach such a high base camp.

This is a beautiful metaphor that I want you to use in the development of the ascension. You have now come to a base camp. In the base camp, you have a foundation or a stabilization. It is an anchor you can return to if you find that you are getting out of sorts. Even if you fall below the base camp, you will have the energy, the spiritual strength, and the will to come back.

This is part of the ascension process. The process not only takes you up to a high level but it also takes groups up to the base point. It is from there that many can go out to the higher realms. When you are in a mountain-climbing experience, then some must stay back to maintain the base camp. They can contact those above and, if necessary, provide supplies to those higher up. Those above can even return to the lower level to recuperate.

Some are already able to reach the higher point and begin their ascension processes. There is also a pre-ascension experience that many are already beginning to attain. They are able to climb this mountain and reach a higher point. From this higher point, they are beginning to experience transformations into the fifth dimension. They are on a wavelength that allows them to vibrate into the fifth and then back into the third dimension. You have not been previously told that you would be able to do this, but some are already accomplishing this through their devotion and their energy work. You will be very pleased to set this up. Do not be afraid. When you are in this vibrational shifting, you can go from one dimensional field to another.

THE STEPS ALONG YOUR DIVINE PATH

The primary work that stabilizes and anchors you is your participation in groups. It is in groups that you are able to meld with other energy. As a group, you will be able to raise those who need to go higher. When you wish to go higher, then you can use the group energy as a foundation.

The ascension is such a beautiful process. It is a process that is designed to fit your needs as you mold yourself to the path. Remember, like climbing a mountain, there are certain difficulties that you could encounter. Some paths will require more ropes, while other paths might be slippery and could cause falls. And some paths might seem impassable right now.

Remember the analogy of the base camp and remember that you can return to that camp at any time. By going back to the base camp, you can gain strength, understanding and knowledge from others who have returned or who have gone there to support you. You cannot maintain yourself on the top of the mountain. As you go into higher spiritual realms, you will need to return. You can return to the base camp and anchor your new energy.

We can talk about your base: The base begins with accepting that you are on a divine path with the understanding that you are opening yourself up to receiving light and etheric energy. You then begin to work with your own energy fields in order to open up to a higher vibration. This opening will enable you to expand your auric field and yourself so that you can understand and receive light and love. You will receive understanding and wisdom. You will also receive divine guidance, including help from your own personal guides.

The next step is accepting that you are a divine being. You are part of the Adam Kadmon.[1] You have the prototype energy within you to be in perfect harmony with the Creator energy. You have within you all of the tools to open up to the highest wisdom. You are divine. When you are divine, you will see yourself as a very beautiful, power-ful, and important person with a mission. The mission can relate in part to your soul experience of development.

Your soul development involves learning certain key lessons and hav-ing key experiences that will enable you to leave the Earthly incarnation process and go into the fifth dimension. If there is leftover work from this incarnation and it appears that you will not complete this work, then you will be attracted by the laws of the universe, the laws of Earth and the laws of the Divine Creator, *B'nai Elohim*,[2] to return. If you are now opening yourself up to the soul lessons you need, then you are completing the task and can move to the next higher base camp.

THE TRACK OF YOUR SOUL PURPOSE

Review your own soul lesson and learn if it focuses, for example, on learning to be more loving or learning to be more aware of your divine purpose. Your lesson could be to learn how to relate to others or to learn how to transcend the good and evil that appear to be occurring on Earth. Your lesson could be to provide teaching to others, such as being a chan-nel or teaching children. Or your lesson could focus on being a caretaker for someone else.

You can also examine the second aspect of your purpose, which is the general purpose. Everything has many levels. The universal experience is multidimensional; thus, your soul purpose is also multidimensional. There are two tracks: the individual track and the general track. The general track can focus on helping others and thus relate to the specific mission in the overall ascension. You also have a specific mission in this work called the ascension, a mission that includes working with light and love. Each of you is yearning to learn how you fit into the divine plan.

There is a divine plan that is unfolding now, and you're part of it. The more you open up to this plan, the more you can open up to your role in it. You will then become a more effective lightworker for others. This becomes an ascending process. Think about your role in the general way, in the overall picture, and then think about your individual role.

Can the individual and the group roles be interwoven?

Definitely. These roles often are interwoven. You need to remember that this is a multilevel path. It is a mission for learning lessons, but it is also a path of service. Eventually, the two paths become so tightly interwoven that you cannot tell the difference between them. The highest ascended masters on your planet are continuously in service while working on their own soul paths.

We who are on a higher level can experience the fifth dimension directly—not on a continuous basis, but only on a temporary, visionary, or insightful aha! level.[3] At that point, we really feel and know in our hearts that there is a higher dimension, and we begin to interface with fifth-dimensional energy. How do we experience this interface? We begin to feel that we are vibrational beings. We begin to understand that as we are vibrational, so is the fifth dimension vibrational. We also feel a sense of clearing. We are able to give up some of our attachments to the Earth plane because we realize that the fifth dimension is where we are destined to be. You are destined to be there too. It is part of your whole unfolding process.

The etheric plane cannot be described in tones and colors that you recognize in the third dimension. The colors are of a deeper tone. Some will feel an overwhelming sense of love and acceptance when they begin to enter the portals and the special entry points for accessing the fifth dimension. At that point, you will be able to meet your guides directly. You also will be able to channel information and access psychic abilities. Even though you are cutting the cords of attachment, you are still in balance on the Earth plane. You will begin to feel a lightness. You will begin to interact with your guides more directly. You will get into deeper meditations, which will include being able to leave your body and move to a higher plane.

You will sense that your lightbody is greater than your physical body, but you will also identify with your physical body. From this higher point of the greater self, you will send light and love back to your physical body. That will enable you to radiate more health and vibrancy.

Is it possible to reach that level during sleep when the mind is more relaxed?

Absolutely. Many have had that experience in their sleep. Sleep is a time when you are totally free of attachments; thus, you are free to practice this ability. One of the goals in the ascension work is to bring the energy from your unconscious mind into your conscious waking experience. Others have talked about the death experience and how important it is to be aware during the dying process. The more aware you are during your death experience, the better it is for your next encounter on the other side.

To answer your question specifically, though, I would say yes, you can receive this information and these experiences in your sleep state. That is good practice. Many of you are more advanced than you think. You do have access to this energy in your sleep. Some will be able to access these experiences in their waking states through trances and then rise to the higher level. They will experience feelings of ecstasy and wholeness, or feelings of oneness, that will be enhanced as they approach the opening into the fifth dimension.

OPEN YOUR HEARTS

I will take you to one more level—the level of the monadic experience.[4] The monadic is the experience that is described as the oneness in which you are able to feel unified with Creator energy. The term monad means "oneness." It must be understood that you are part of the monad. We come from the same Source. You are able to merge with this oneness, yet at the same time, you will not experience giving up your sense of self.

We will work with you on enhancing this monadic experience. I will use one of the channeled Hebrew sounds, *Elohim*[5] (God, the Creator energy). When you listen to this beautiful sound, it is hoped you will be able to experience the oneness and your relationship to the monad. Repeat this word: "*Elohim . . . Elohim . . . Elohim.*"

At the monadic level, you can open your heart fully. The key to the monadic experience and to integrating that experience with the ascension process lies in your ability to open up your hearts. Then you can feel and directly experience this wonderful monadic energy. All of you are able to experience this; it is part of your coded structure. This structure is described in the book *The Book of Knowledge: The Keys of Enoch* by James J. Hurtak. You are genetically set up to participate in the celestial realms, including experiencing the celestial music. This is your birthright. Follow it and it will lead you to your true home.

It is on this higher level that you can feel your chakras opening very wide. Your heart chakra will vibrate especially strongly. The fact that you can come into this level easily is a sign of your accomplishments as lightbeings. I encourage you to stay at this level in your meditations.

Notes:

1. "Adam Kadmon" is the Hebrew term for the primordial man. It has been described as the prototype of the first being to emerge after the beginning of Creation. The Adam Kadmon serves as an intermediary between the Tao and the world to come. It is said that all of the souls of man were originally in Adam Kadmon. This concept is to be distinguished from Adam and Eve.

2. The name that describes the Creator in the first chapter of Genesis is *Elohim*. It is a word with a plural ending, -im, but it is used as a singular noun when applied to Israel's God. The *B'nai Elohim* is referred to in Genesis 5:6 and is translated as the "divine beings." Others translate it as the "sons of God." This name refers to possible supermen of great strength who were supposedly the offspring of unions between gods and men. In J. J. Hurtak's *The Book of Knowledge: The Keys of Enoch* they are defined as the paradise sons who dispatched judgment and hierarchical education and choose the "selected seeds." They also are special Elohistic extensions of the Father, expressing the Father's infinite purpose and love.

3. "Aha!" is a psychological term often used to describe the emotion a person feels after having a divine insight or idea—an epiphany.

4. The original, elemental creative force. "The Beginning was in the Totality, and from the Totality sprang forth that energy from which began the Monad." June Singer, *Androgyny: Toward a New Theory of Sexuality* (Garden City, NY: Anchor Books, 1977), 224.

5. Phonetically, the word is pronounced El-oh-heem.

CHAPTER 7

KARMA AND GRACE DURING THE ASCENSION

Sananda

I think it is important to review what the ascension is—where we have been and where we are going. It has been an interesting unfolding since the announcement of the ascension. Many have adapted quickly to the idea and eagerly anticipated its arrival. Some have been foolish and disregarded their responsibilities, expecting to be removed immediately. They have been deeply disappointed. Others have continued the work in deep devotion. They accepted hardships and are prepared for the difficult work ahead.

You cannot speak about who you are and why you are here unless you discuss karma and participation in the ascension. You can do a tremendous amount of work and release an enormous karmic load in a brief time. In this short lifetime, you can now accomplish what could have taken many lifetimes. When the end is near, you accelerate by working harder; you want to do as much as possible before the ascension arrives. This is part of human nature and is a positive development.

Realizing the ascension means the acknowledgment of your multidimensional existence. You are a multidimensional being existing physically in the third dimension, which is a slow and dense dimension. When something happens in this dimension, the result is not immediate. It takes time.

OVERCOMING KARMIC BLOCKS

You might be responding now, karmically, to events earlier in your life. For example, you could have been exposed to radiation when you were younger, and it could now be affecting you physically. Such a physical problem could be caused by events earlier in your life and have nothing to do with your recent activities as a lightworker. Now, however, you have the ability to focus your healing in ways that you could not have comprehended when you were younger. Use these deeper resources within to heal yourselves.

Exposure to radiation is one example of accumulated karma from this lifetime. Another example might focus on the way you think of yourselves. As you think, so it manifests. At times you can avoid negative thoughts, but some negative thoughts might stay with you even though they did not manifest immediately. Perhaps you think you have released those thought patterns, and then a major disturbance occurs in your life and seems totally unrelated to your light work. In all other aspects of your life, you have been very fortunate and devoted, but suddenly you have a major block, and you don't know where it came from. You don't want to deal with it, but you are being forced to do so with a hard push.

Such an event is not unkind. Don't interpret this as: "I am not going to make it." I want you to understand that some of the blocks that occur are not necessarily the results of thoughts or patterns that you have experienced since your introduction to the ascension. Blocks originating from earlier events do not necessarily mean that you are currently thinking in a wrong way or that you are now unworthy. You have not failed and become somehow undeserving of the ascension. Please understand this. Don't continue with that kind of thinking, my friends. In part, it is that type of thinking that originally fostered the block.

When you are blocked and suffering from a problem that seems unsolvable, suddenly your ability for self-love all goes out the window. You are being tested to see if you can still love yourselves deeply. Self-love will get you through your block. It all comes down to this simple expression of wisdom. It is easy to practice when things are going well. I am very encouraged that you are aware of this lesson and are beginning to understand it on a deeper level. You have a wonderful opportunity now to make advancements. If you start with the premise of self-love and self-understanding, then you can process any karmic problem.

Do not worry about the seemingly slow progress; compare it to lifetimes. Remember when we talked about the ascension years ago [in 1993], and we discussed accelerated karma? We talked about accomplishing things that might otherwise have taken several lifetimes or more. All were eager. "Yes! Yes!" you said, "Bring it on. This is fantastic! I am ready. I can take on karma for five more lifetimes if it means that I am close to ascending and close to transcending this planet. Of course I am ready!" Do you remember that type of thinking? Now are you just as eager to volunteer?

You need to respect yourselves for the paths you are on. It is a monumental task to go through many of these karmic problems. There are periods of grace and smooth sailing. It cannot be all hard work. There needs to be a time of letting down. Many made the mistake of letting down in the beginning. You are now in a place where you have integrated the major hurdle or the huge first step.

Keep a positive attitude and an openness about the work you are doing. It might not be developing in the way you had expected it to. Please understand that your own guides and teachers are involved in this process and are guiding you with your higher selves in agreement.

THE I AM PRESENCE

Now let me go into the question of when the ascension will occur. You have heard the guides speak about their refusal to give a time and date. You know how difficult it is for someone to predict when an event will occur on this plane. The reason for this is that people do not take into account things that have occurred in earlier times.

To predict accurately, you would have to access so much information that you truly would need a computer to process it. Occurrences you are now seeing on the Earth plane could be the result of events dating back to the Middle Ages. Some incidents happening now are the result of events of 2,000 years ago. For example, people began at that time to formulate religious beliefs that are affecting the planet now. Even though those formulations were based on limited knowledge, they were accepted then and have been instituted, deeply affecting the process of your whole culture.

We are finished with the first part of the initiation phase; the initiation of the planetary ascension has been completed. Many of you have participated in it completely, while some are still just beginning to be exposed to it. Because of the work that has been done by so many lightworkers—the beautiful publications, lectures, and speeches of many beautiful channels—the groundwork has been laid successfully. I think it was a job well done! I am pleased with the devotion that has been evidenced in the spreading of this beautiful concept. The lightworkers have made an impact. There is now a solid base now of workers, knowledge, and transformational awareness that has infiltrated the planet. This is a very positive outcome. Some catastrophes have even been prevented by thought patterns and work on the grids by lightworkers.

Just as there are going to be three waves of ascension, so there will be three phases of the ascension process. The second part of the ascension will not be harder than the first. It is not necessarily true that you have to experience hardship. There may be hard work, but your attitude toward the work can change. Many are already able to experience lightness and ease. They are able to accomplish more work than they ever thought possible.

It is important that you know who you are. To ascend, you must be conscious of your multidimensional self and of your I Am presence—*Eh'yeh asher Eh'yeh* (I Am That I Am). This is your connection to your transformation and to your multidimensional self. When you repeat those phrases and feel them within your heart chakras, then you open deeply. You experience the wonderfulness of yourselves. Do not think that this is selfish. It is actually selfless. You are selfless in your I Am presence. You are above yourselves. You are above your egos. You are even above this lifetime. You are above your deaths. You are unified with eternity and with the Creator energy. You have direct access to it; it is pretty powerful. That's who you are: You are that powerful. You are that beautiful. You are multidimensional.

You can access the I Am self through many different techniques. We have introduced you to the concept of the lightbody. That is the aspect of you that is able, willing, and eager to come down to you from its point of highest vibration and highest contact with the Creator energy. You all have lightbodies. You can all access them. You all can bring energy down from them. This is part of being a vessel of light. This is part of your light work. Fill your physical presence with this light. This is what we have called anchoring. This is what we call acceleration on the energetic level. You all can do that. Call on your lightbodies. You do not even need to use the Hebrew words; you can use the English words: "I Am That I Am." This is what brought Moses into alignment with the Creator energy. When these words were spoken to him, it was an instant transformation. He was opened. You also are now opening deeply. When you repeat these words again and again, there will be a time when you will open as deeply as Moses did. Sense it now! Sense your lightbodies. [Sings.] *Eh'yeh asher Eh'yeh.*

GRACE ENERGY

Bring this energy into your physical bodies. Bring this energy into your lives and onto your paths from this point forward. It is not just an energy to bring you into oneness and joy. It is that, but it is also an energy that you can continually flush through your lifetimes from now on. It is an energy acceleration. It can remove karma in a heightened way. Move the energy now through your physical bodies, through your lives in all aspects, in all the roles you play, in all the different places you go. Think of them now and bring the light in.

Some people say that grace will supersede the need to work with karma from this life and past lives to transmute it and balance it. Is that accurate?

This is a very complex question. I will try to give a simple answer. The karma will not be erased; rather, it will be balanced. It will be accelerated so that you can transmute yourselves. For example, suppose you were to have a negative karma about balance and you walked out the door and tripped on a step. You could then say that you needed to learn a lesson about balance. Grace can be offered to you, and in meditation you might receive this message: "Be very careful when you leave the house tonight. You could fall and hurt your ankle and have much unhappiness about that. But that will not happen if you learn balance. Are you ready to learn balance now?" If you answer yes, then you have to learn to walk in balance through all facets of your life.

Because you agreed to learn that lesson, you can then go on without breaking your ankle, thus bypassing a negative karma. Six months from now, you might forget this lesson. Something then has to happen to remind you, so it would be arranged that you sprain your ankle slightly and are thrown off balance for a day or two. In meditation you would then say, "Aha! I remember when I talked with Sananda six months ago. I got that lesson! I need to be more balanced."

In this example, the grace energy was successful the first time. You got off the path a little bit, but it wasn't necessary for you to break your ankle. If you hadn't learned the lesson, then the original grace would not have been useful, and then you might even have had to break your knee the next time in order to integrate the lesson. I am using this example to explain that grace is an interactive energy. It would not be for your highest good to have grace if you did not balance and integrate your learning.

Look at grace as a possible opening and a chance to learn and integrate lessons. Grace energy is continuously available. You can call on the grace energy for yourself. Yes, there is grace for the planet. Many of our American Indian friends have been very strong in bringing that energy of grace into the planet.

YOU HAVE MANY NAMES

I heard that grace is available and that it can be called on and used. Integration is very important afterward, but grace might be recognized by us as accelerated learning.

Yes. This implies that a negative event was about to occur, but you will now be spared from it because you have accelerated your learning. Everything has a price in the universe, and the price you pay for grace is learning. When you have learned and integrated the lesson, that's the payoff to us, the spiritual hierarchy, and the universe.

What was the name that those people called you just then?

Sananda. It is a galactic name that I have used. I have many names, just as you do. Do you think this is the only name you have?

I'm used to using just one.

If we were to use one of your other names, it might open up a memory or two. It would create a vibrational experience that would bring in more light.

Do you like to be called by that name?

Yes, especially in this context. It is easier for many to accept. You must admit, the other name has lots of overtones. People bring lots of expectations. I want people to understand that this is a new era that we are in. I want people to understand that we are co-equals. You do not worship one over another. We are part of a galactic race. This is part of our heritage in the Milky Way. This is your home. There are others from other parts of the galaxy that are your brothers and sisters. Even the seeding of this planet has come from an extra-planetary source.

I haven't been exposed to those kinds of ideas. I am open to any explanation anyone might want to venture at this point.

I am not asking you to believe it. I am not asking you to say that is the truth. Simply allow the concept to merge in your intellect. You do not have to believe it. Forget I ever said it to you. Forget this part of the lecture. [Laughs.] By using the name Sananda, I am also suggesting that I am a galactic force and a galactic energy as well. This energy is more than just planetary.

This has been very moving. You are obviously very sensitive and very wise and very knowledgable. I respect that in you.

Flattery will get you everywhere with the channel, but it will get you nowhere with me.

CHAPTER 8

Belief Systems and Ascension: Don't Look Back!

Sananda

I want to directly talk about myself and my relationship to you. I want to talk about how my existence fits in with the scheme of things. You know, for many people on the planet, the fact that I now exist and am talking to you is very controversial. The fact that my name[1] has been changed is difficult for many people to accept. It is even difficult for you [the channel] to accept that I am speaking through you. The whole concept of the Messiah needs to be explored as well. That is a broad subject, and we will not be able to cover it as deeply as I would like to, but I will attempt to place it in perspective.

Your Perspective on Belief Systems

The first thing I want to tell you definitively is that no one on the Earth plane now has all of the information about what is occurring or what has occurred. You speak about my existence 2,000 years ago based on the interpretations and observations of others. There were no video cameras present! Even now when events occur, news becomes distorted.

Secondly, each of you has a particular perspective depending on religious beliefs or a different cultural background. Your belief systems[2] are very precious to you. Indeed, one of the inviolable rules of growth in the universe is that we will not violate your belief systems. It is very important that all belief systems be respected. For example, you know that when people die, many interact with beings conforming to their own view of death. If you believe in the angels, then you are met by the angels. Some say there must be only one belief system that is right. I cannot answer yes or no to that. When you say what you believe, you must add the statement: "This is from my perspective." Rest assured that is the most important perspective to have.[3]

Even your beliefs about the ascension, which you feel you perhaps understand fairly well, can be problematic. When the ideas of the ascension were taught to you, it was important that those ideas were brought forth in a way that would conform to your belief systems. Ascension might even extend some of your belief systems. It had to be presented in such a way that you could tolerate it and grow with it. Some have had trouble because the ascension has not happened according to *their* timetable. The timetable we are operating from is different.

Some have asked if a particular person is now the representative of the Christ. The answer is this: We are not going to say that anyone is a direct emissary on this plane right now! Each of you must determine that for yourself. It is important that you have completely free access to belief systems. This is the ultimate test of your free will—to exercise your belief systems. Before you criticize another person's belief system or another group's belief system, remember and understand that you will not have all the information until you have passed on to the other realms.

There Is More than One Way

For my friends who are Jewish, I want to say a few words. It is important that you understand I do exist. Some ask, "Are you Jewish?" If a space brother were to talk to you—assume that he existed in a form that was alien to your views of what a physical entity should look like—you might have difficulty believing in, accepting, or even tolerating his presence. Likewise, in my time, if someone were to talk about religion or spirituality, it was most acceptable to come through as a Jew. That was the time when there was spiritual awareness and presence in that "garment."

People ask if it was my intention to start a new religion. Again I will say that it is not my role to judge how people interpret my life. There were so many different perceptions. My message was to present spirit and eternal life and to say that there is a way you can attain them. If you wish, you can come through me, and I will take you that way. Other belief systems can also accommodate you if you do not wish to come through me. I am not here to say that all must come through me. All can come through me who wish to. Perhaps you know a better way for yourself. There are many other beautiful religions on this planet as well as throughout the galaxy.

When it is perceived that only one person has the answer, the "right" perception, then hatred and violence can be engendered, such as the hatred and violence that we are now witnessing. When one has a perspective and says, "This is *the* perspective and you must follow it!" then violence can result. You do not want to be told what to believe.

Do you think that I would come here and say, "This is the one way, and you must follow it; I am the only way, and you must come through me"? Do you see that in your Old Testament or in the New Testament? How would you respond if I were to say to you, "You must come through me"? You would think, "This is a totalitarian leader speaking."

Why did others experience it that way? Look at your own human nature. Look at the energy placed here from the Orion culture and the interaction of the galactic forces that have been involved in interbreeding. You understand it is not a conflict that has occurred only on this planet; it has occurred on other planets as well. Other planets in your galaxy believed that they had the "right" way.

The way to be is to *be*. Is this not what *Eh'yeh asher Eh'yeh* is? I Am That I Am. I Will Be That I Will Be. All can approach from their own perspectives and love if they have the right heart opening. Those who have exclusive approaches are not coming totally from the heart; they come with critical minds.

BELIEVE IN THE CREATOR

Now I want to discuss the concept of the Messiah—the idea that there is a being who will save the planet. I tell you that there is a leader of the ascension, although that leader perhaps does not conform to your conception of what the Messiah is. From your perspective, you have a conception that the Messiah should save the world. You might think the best way for the Messiah to act is to come down miraculously and wave a wand so that suddenly all is transformed: Those who are evil die and go to hell, others rise into spaceships, and some think it over and accept the ascension later. Perhaps that is how you conceive of it. I am not criticizing that. I am just saying that it is a vision from your perspective. But remember, you do not have all the necessary information about how a Messiah should be.

What would be for the overall good of all on the planet? Even those who are not in the light should not be robbed of their karma. What is the essence of the meaning of the Messiah? Does it mean that someone must save a person from his own experiences? Can people circumvent karma and immediately transform into the higher dimensions without paying their karmic debts? What if I told you that you can do exactly that with my assistance? You have within you the ability to be your own savior!

Some might say, "Aha, now Sananda is saying each of us is the savior. This is more blasphemy!" I have come—and I did come—to show you how to be. This is a gift. I am not here to ask you to make a decision about the Messiah. The true basis for judging whether or not a person has been helped focuses on how he feels inside.

Your perspective and your conception of the ascension have been developed on insufficient information. Even what we and others have been telling you is limited. Do not feel that you have the final word on the ascension. For example, no one on the Earth plane knows when it will occur. No one can say exactly what sound will be used or how everyone will respond. There are many unknowns. It would not be in your highest interest to know. If you knew that you would ascend tomorrow, then perhaps you would not continue the beautiful work you are doing now.

People say, "Make a decision, make a choice about religion, and tell us which belief is correct." I tell you this: The belief you need to have is in the Creator. I offer a way for you to follow, but there are other approaches that have been and will be available to you. They all meet in the same place that I am going to take you. Have an open heart, and don't be critical of other belief systems. Have a total openness about the ascension. Remember also that you do not have all the information about your higher self or about your role on this planet right now. Many of you will not have that information until the proper time.

No One Has All the Answers

It grieves me to see such pain and suffering on the planet. It grieves me to see pain and suffering over my name or over any other belief system. This is a very tragic development on this planet, and it is rampant. You will find that in the Pleiades and on other planets it is not occurring.

You are free to explore your belief systems and act them out to the highest degree possible without condemnation and without fear. You will find that this is the highest gift of spirit—to experience what you believe. When you can practically experience what you believe, you will find out immediately whether those beliefs are good for you or not. If you have a bad belief about yourself, it can take some time to manifest on this plane. On a higher level, it will manifest instantaneously. The adjustments will be magnificently quick.

I say to you that when you evaluate others, remember that no one on this planet at this time has all the answers. *No one* has all of the information. Be careful of any who say that they do have all the answers, because by the fact of their existence here and their manifestation in incarnation, they have become limited. This limitation is part of the incarnation process that I too experienced in my lifetime. You know the trials and tribulations I had to go through and the doubts I had to experience when I was growing up. The "deal" was that when I came here, I would go through everything a mortal man would experience. That was the task. That meant being cut off or experiencing the illusion of being cut off. Truly, my coming was not to condemn any belief. You never heard me say that I had all the answers. That is the place of our Father.

Someone said, "You and the Father are one." This is true, but understand that manifestation created a separation. Compare this to the concept of the *Shekhinah*[4] in the *Kaballah*. The separation allows the manifestation. This is a very critical point in understanding the energy of the *Shekhinah* and of the Christ. Through the separation comes the manifestation. It becomes a split. That is how this world was created.

This idea goes back to the concept of the sin of Adam—which, from my perspective, was not a sin but a separation that was necessary for the creation of the species. The so-called original sin was, from my perspective, the evolutionary step necessary for the existence of the species. Without separation, there would have been no drive, no instinct for survival; the species would have simply remained merged. The Creator Father/Mother energy wanted the existence of the species, so the separation occurred. It was not a sin; it was a trauma. I suggest that original sin be redefined as "original trauma." It was the trauma of the separation that created the hardships.

WE ARE MAKING PREPARATIONS FOR YOU

As you approach the ascension energies and as you approach the understanding of my existence and of that of the other guides, such as my dear friend Ashtar, understand that you can approach this trauma of Adam and Eve and know that you are moving toward unification. That will lead you very directly to the ascension.

In the context of spiritual development, I think it's important that you understand what is about to occur. When you consider the ascension as a process, then you must realize that it is a cumulative event, an event that does not occur in isolation. Instead, it is a process that has unfolded and is now reaching a culmination in your lifetime.

My role in the ascension is to coordinate it and to ensure that it occurs smoothly and effectively and is open to as many souls as possible. It is true that the ascension is an event that offers unprecedented outreach to many souls. I ask you to consider the ascension as an energy of outreach. We on the side of divine spirit and white light are making a special effort to help those who are moving in the direction of spiritual transformation and enlightenment.

You might believe that you have not earned this spiritual gift. Perhaps you might consider that you have not really reached the necessary spiritual attainments. You might even think you need ten or twenty more lifetimes to accomplish sufficient spiritual awakening and transformation. Yet because of the outreach on your side, you now have the ability to plug into a spiritual electric current that will melt many dense thoughts, karmic ties and negativities that might require another lifetime or two to unfold. By connecting into our outreach current, you can transform many low-level energies into the energy of ascension.

I am awaiting orders to begin the ascension. It will not occur until the minute is exactly perfect. It will not occur until a certain alignment takes place—an alignment in your physical plane and also an alignment of energies that are coming from the galactic core. This alignment can be viewed as an opening that allows those who are spiritually prepared and ready to accept the process of ascension to actually travel through a specially designed tunnel of transformation. I use the word "tunnel" because it might fit your understanding of how it is possible to move from one dimension to another. You may also visualize it as a spaceship bringing you up.

Those who are under my command will have the assistance of Ashtar, the angelic hosts and others who will be ready and able to help you along the path and onto the other side. It is important that you understand that I have chosen others who will be there to help you move along. Although you might "evaporate" instantaneously from your physical presence on planet Earth, you will still have a journey to take through the ascension currents. You will have various areas to traverse, and it will be important to continue without stopping.

You could view the ascension as an experience in which you will receive sudden enlightenment—an instantaneous awareness and brilliance about all that is occurring on the entire planet. With that awareness, you might feel at that time that you want to stop to enjoy and participate in that beautiful energy; however, it is required that you continue to move along. Some might begin the ascension and then try to stop and take a peek over the mountain, if I may use this analogy. Perhaps you might want to view those who were left behind to see how they are experiencing things. In that second of translation, you will immediately be put into an extra-pyramidal time frame that compares to a longer period of time transpiring on the Earth plane.

For example, if in that second you were to stop the process for any reason and look back, you might note that weeks or months have gone by. You would be interested in how others are adapting to your absence. You might be interested in how the world is progressing now. You may have thoughts from your ego such as, "Boy, I'm glad I'm not there any more. It's getting pretty heavy down there. I don't think I would want to participate in that." These thoughts are similar to what you would feel knowing that someone was caught in a snowstorm in another part of the country.

KEEP YOUR FOCUS FORWARD

So I am instructing you to not stop and to not take a look, as normal and as human as that might be. Looking back is evidence of a continuing ego attachment, because you compare yourself to where you were before. That is why it is so important in your preparation for the ascension that you practice ego release. Use the Sword of Michael,[5] as Ashtar and others have called it, to cut your ego attachments.

I want you to have a successful transformation and ascension. That is why so many of my good comrades and friends will be available to help you. You may call on them as your guides. You will recognize them immediately as your friends who are under my command. We are responsible for leading you into the next dimension. You are coming as our special guests. We are preparing a table for you, and we have a special entry place for your spiritual arrival. Please keep your focus on that goal rather than trying to make sense of events that are transpiring as you leave.

This focus is important, because some of you are looking for a particular time when ascension will occur. Some are looking for a particular moment, such as when there is much darkness and terror and many calamities on the planet. Then perhaps you picture that you will leave, escaping from the darkness that is occurring. I understand this attitude, and I appreciate it. Yet I ask you again to consider not focusing necessarily on the idea of,

"This will be my escape." The ascension is not an escape. Using the word "escape" is still using the terminology of the ego.

The ascension is a true transformation that occurs at the right moment. You must have faith that it will occur when it is most propitious for all involved. You need not focus on a particular time, nor do you need to wait for a particular chain of circumstances. Having said this, I realize at the same time that there will be a chain of circumstances that will occur. There will be a period of darkness soon that will pre-establish that the ascension is about to occur. I am saying: Do not become attached to those occurrences in any way. Work on becoming detached, and understand that your role is that of a lightbeing.

I am ensuring that the proper guides are aligned with those souls in need. I will also coordinate reports from the various guides and the workers, which will be used in higher council to consider the proper alignments and whether or not to step up certain energy levels. The information we receive helps us pump certain energies and awareness down to you. It is a delicate process. Ascension requires a directed energy of "overloadedness," or tolerance, so that we are sure that you are receiving as much energy as you can possibly accept.

ASCENSION HAS BEGUN

There have been many different metaphors for the ascension. For example, you have heard the ascension referred to as the translation. Each metaphor in its own right describes a portion of this reality that you call the ascension. It is like a diamond that has many facets. Do not think that you have the final answer or the final facet of the ascension. There are other aspects of the ascension that you are perhaps not aware of. I am only asking that you maintain light from your perspective. Others may come from another perspective that you might not agree with or understand, but other perspectives can be just as valid.

I am not asking that you become messiahs for others or that you convert others. Others are being worked on by their guides. I am asking you to participate 100 percent from your own side of the diamond, which will bring you into harmony with the ascension energy. Please understand that the ascension has already begun, because the outreach and the transformation process have begun. Do not necessarily conceive of it as one aspect that will occur at one place and time. Understand that it is a process and a transformation that is continually occurring. It has roots in a time before it began, and it will continue until the actual transformation when you will leave the planet.

Your preparation, studies, and light work are part of your ascension. Realize this now. Realize that it has begun; the seeds have been planted in your mind. You are already participating, preparing, and releasing.

I appreciate the statement about not having to know everything about the ascension. That would be so overwhelming.

Again, all I am asking is that you know about your side of the ascension, whether it is the side of the lightworkers or the side of the space brothers or another side. This is a large enough understanding for you. When you reach the higher understanding, your portion of this diamond will fit exactly into the overall diamond. You will connect instantaneously with all others. It is a fit that you are working toward.

There seems to have been a lessening of interest in or enthusiasm for the ascension. Perhaps some think it will not occur because they are not getting enough encouragement, but I assure you that it will occur. You have received the seeds, and it is a continuous process on a timetable that is suited to your needs. In actuality, that means a date is not given. Were you to be given a date, you would become attached to that date, which would encourage ego attachment. To fully participate in the ascension, you need to release ego attachment. Thank you for your enthusiasm and dedication.

Notes:

1. In the *Kaballah*, Sananda is known as Joshua ben Miriam of Nazareth, which translates as Joshua, son of Mary of Nazareth. For more information, see Z'ev ben Shimon Halevi, *School of the Soul: Its Paths and Pitfalls* (York Beach, ME: Red Wheel/Weiser, 1993), 137.
2. In this context, the term "belief systems" refers to major religious or spiritual systems such as Christianity, Judaism, and so forth.
3. That is, to acknowledge that your beliefs are from your own perspective.
4. *Shekhinah*: In Hebrew, the Divine Mother. *Shekhinah* is the frequently used Talmudic term denoting the visible and audible manifestation of God's presence on Earth. In its ultimate concept, it stands for an independent feminine entity, the Divine Mother. For more information, see Raphael Patai, *The Hebrew Goddess* (Detroit, MI: Wayne State University Press, 1978), 96.
5. Archangel Michael's etheric sword can help cut through ego and karmic ties at the moment of ascension, which will allow you to move on quickly into the next dimension.

CHAPTER 9

ADAM-EVE KADMON[1]

Rabbi Hayyim Vital[2]

It is important that you understand that the *Kaballah* means "to receive." It is an evolving receiving. So if you compare the *Kaballah* in the sixth century to the *Kaballah* in the twentieth century, you will see differences. The time has changed. Many things are different now on your planet. The universal laws are the same, but there are new variations. Even as you are progressing in this incarnation, you are constantly making adjustments in your psyche so that you can be in better attunement. Likewise, when you review the whole body called the *Kaballah*, there are adjustments that need to be made.

ADJUSTMENTS FOR THE ASCENSION

The first adjustment I will speak about is a very shocking one for many: The *Kaballah* itself has been revealed from a planetary source beyond your solar system. The *Kaballah* as an energy force was brought to this planet partly through the efforts of the Pleiadians. They had been working with the energy that you know as the *Zohar*, the special supernal light that has been studied for many periods of time outside of your solar system. The *Zohar* was introduced through various revelations as a necessity. It was important that these seeds of understanding be planted within the race. Remember that the *Kaballah* is beyond this planet and has been studied throughout this galaxy and beyond.

The second adjustment focuses on understanding that the energy of receiving is also an energy of transformation. When you receive this light, the light of the *Zohar*, in the normal physical density that you call third-dimensional reality, you are transforming yourself to unify with your lightbody. In order to unify with your lightbody, you must go through transformations. When you receive the Zohar energy, it enables you to reunite with your highest lightbody.

Adam Kadmon represents the perfected soul light. It is the Zohar soul in perfect unity with the light of the *Zohar*. This is the ultimate unification of the self. The Zohar light is so powerful that you must be specially prepared. For example, you might need to go through repeated incarnations to attain the proper harmony before you can reunite with that light. Then when you are in that light, you can merge with Adam Kadmon. Each of you has a part in Adam Kadmon. That is where this beautiful concept of reunification comes in.

The third adjustment is found in J. J. Hurtak's *The Book of Knowledge: Keys of Enoch*. The transformation occurring now is a planetary experience. We are speaking of the reunification or the restoration[3] on a planetary basis, not just on an individual or group basis. Keep in the forefront of your consciousness not only your own healing but also the planetary healing. Keep in mind not only your own ascension but also the planetary ascension. We are working together with the Brotherhood. It is for all to join hands and open their hearts together in this wonderful unification.

There is a final adjustment or correction. You are now in the stage of your evolutionary development in which you are beginning to accept both aspects within yourself, the male and the female. When the feminine side comes into full play with the male side and when the male side comes into full play with the feminine side, then you move closer to the energy of God.

From our perspective, I will say that we wish the energy were referred to as "Adam-Eve Kadmon" instead of "Adam Kadmon." It sounds as if it is only the male side when you say Adam Kadmon. You know that Adam Kadmon is really male and female together, not just male. Adam-Eve Kadmon is a new term you can use to make sure that all understand what we are talking about.

HEALING WITH BLUE LIGHT

When uniting with that energy of Adam-Eve Kadmon, you can use that energy to be of a higher vibration. You may go back and unite with the Adam-Eve Kadmon energy again and again. It is like being recharged. This charge is so powerful that all who can approach the Adam-Eve Kadmon energy receive an acceleration. You know that the genetic codes need to be stimulated and awakened.

As you are unfolding, you can go into deeper levels within yourself. You can stimulate deeper and more complex levels to unlock these codes. When you unite with Adam-Eve Kadmon energies, you will gain access to your true multidimensional and androgynous nature. You will also gain direct memories of your previous incarnations as well as instructions about ascension. You will receive instructions on a daily basis, and you will begin to serve as a healer.

I want to talk with you about different rays of light, including the blue light. This is a healing light that has rays of energy that are very valuable for you. Your sky is blue. You are in a planetary system that has a unique energy of blueness in it. This blue light will have a great influence on the ascension. The blue light has an energy wave that you are very open to now.

Use the blue for protection and acceleration. If there is one color that is really earthly and healing at this time, it is blue. As we move through different time periods, you will find that there will be different colors that will have more power than others. For the period we are now in, blue will have a very powerful effect on you.

Let us speak about the energy of *Baruch*.[4] This energy is very powerful, and it is another force you have to work with. Simply the sound *"Baruch"* has a power of manifestation of holiness [sings]: *"Baruch."* As you are moving through your day, you may repeat that word for every gift you are experiencing. It is as if you are thanking the Creator and multiplying your gifts as you are receiving them.

ACCESS MANIFESTED ENERGY

The concept of the image of God and the image of our Father/Mother God has been a very controversial topic in the *Kaballah*.[5] You are correct in interpreting that you are made in the likeness of our Mother and Father. Some have said that God cannot have a form. I say to you that God can indeed have a form; of course the Creator can have a form. Father/Mother God can also appear through emissaries and manifest. To say that there is no manifestation, that he/she is unmanifested, does not make sense. The Creator can do all. To say that there is something that you are able to do that our Creator cannot do (manifest) does not make sense.

From your perspective, however, you cannot simply reach the unmanifested aspect of the Creator.[6] I say this to you as a Kaballist: Why would you focus on the unmanifested aspect in the third dimension when there is so much work to be done in interacting with the manifested side? There is so much energy you can immerse in on the manifested level. You did not come into this incarnation to experience the unmanifested, did you? You came to experience the manifested side. This is the challenge.

There is, though, an aspect of the Creator that is unmanifested. You cannot experience that aspect because you do not understand how an existence can be unmanifested. As you move up the dimensional ladder and begin to approach the seventh and eighth levels, you will better grasp an understanding of this paradox.

The specific manifested aspect of the Creator energy on this planet will help to magnify your transformation. Your Adam-Eve Kadmon genetic structure enables you to experience the manifested Creator energy. You are able to have the experience of the Creator on the level you are open to. This means that if you are open to having it through Sananda, then that is what you will experience. If you are open to experiencing it on another level, then that could happen. There are so many different aspects by which you can experience this energy.

By accessing the Adam-Eve Kadmon, you can reach a true unification. When you are able to unite with this energy, you then form a harmony. The anchoring of this harmonious energy in the third dimension leads to the ascension, which in the *Kaballah* is also referred to as the restoration.

There is going to be an overwhelming power on this planet. Even though the lightworkers are outnumbered, their experience will be a catalyst for the transformation. This is wonderful! More are opening up to the energy, and the first step is to receive more light and more of the oneness energy through Adam-Eve Kadmon. Do not shy away from that experience. Strive for the experience of the Zohar light and for the unification of yourself with Adam-Eve Kadmon.

Notes:

1. This is an expansion of Adam Kadmon, which means primordial man. Adam-Eve Kadmon is the primordial man-woman.
2. Hayyim Vital was a Kaballist and rabbi who lived from AD 1543 to AD 1620 in Safed, Palestine. Vital was particularly close to Luria, the foremost Kaballist of his time, and he was his principal and most outstanding disciple.
3. Restoration in the *Kaballah* is referred to as *tikkun*, or the divine restoration of the cosmos. Each human act is described as either aiding or impeding this process. Note the relationship between restoration and ascension. The vessels holding the light from the Creator were broken, and it is the task of humans to help restore the broken vessels.
4. *Baruch* is the Hebrew word for "blessed," often used in referring to the Creator.
5. Biblical monotheism is tied to the imageless worship of God. However, to discuss the Creator, one must necessarily use the imagery of the created world. For more information, see Gershom Scholem, *On the Mystical Shape of the Godhead* (Jerusalem: Schocken Books, 1991), 15.
6. This is referred to as the *Ain Sof*, also spelled *Ayn Sof* or *Ein Sof* in *Kaballah*, or "that without end." It is sometimes compared to the great Tao. *Ain Sof* is the absolute perfection in which there are no distinctions and no differentiations. It does not reveal itself in a way that makes knowledge of its nature possible. It also is identified with the "cause of all causes." In the Kaballistic system, light symbolism is commonly used in connection with *Ain Sof*.

CHAPTER 10

UNLOCKING YOUR GENETIC CODES

Archangel Metatron[1]

L et us speak with you about the Keys of Enoch and about the process of unlocking your genetic codes. The whole Enoch tradition and the working of the *merkava*[2] help you unlock the codes so that you may access higher states of consciousness. You cannot directly enter these states of awareness until the proper codes, preparations, and releases have been completed. This is for your protection. If you were to enter higher realms without doing the necessary preparations—that is, without entering into an altered state—then you would find yourself becoming dissociated and confused, and harm could come to you.

These codes are for your own protection. It is like going into a bank and wanting to open your safe-deposit box. Only those knowing the right combinations can enter and take the valuables from the safe. In the same way, in order to enter into the higher realms, you must be able to open your safe.

Some of the works you have been studying give you information about the codes. You have information about the codes in the Old Testament and in the New Testament as well. Many of these codes are based on prayers, and many of the prayers have certain sounds that will enable you to go into an altered state of consciousness. One of the most useful Hebrew prayers you can use to enter into a higher state of consciousness is: "*Kadosh, Kadosh, Kadosh Adonai Tzevaoth*" (Holy, Holy, Holy is the Lord of Hosts).[3] We will work with you on this prayer. The words and their meanings are important; it is the whole experience of working with the sound[4] and understanding what you are trying to do. As you use the sounds, hold the attitude that you are accessing another state of consciousness. As you chant the sounds, you will find that you can transform your awareness and enter into a different realm.

While chanting this prayer, you might feel as if you are in a tunnel. You might feel streams of light moving through the tunnel. You might even find that you are accelerating through this tunnel, reaching out for a higher realm. In the realm into which you have expanded your consciousness, you can receive information and energy that will be healing. Then feel yourself coming out of the other end of the tunnel. Now picture yourself perhaps in a garden or in an open field where the colors are extremely bright.

AN ENERGY OF TRANSFORMATION

The focus of the whole Enoch tradition is in the phrase "I Am That I Am."[5] This means that you prepare yourself by aligning with the I Am energy. This alignment will enable you to move into the higher realms. The I Am presence is the most sacred presence because it is your center. From your center, you can resonate with the center of the universe and with the Creator Spirit.

Now we will use the sounds of *Eh'yeh asher Eh'yeh* to help move you into the space of the I Am presence. You will first unite your own energies with your I Am presence. You cannot unite with the I Am presence of the Father and Mother Spirit until you are in alignment with your own I Am presence. Then you can receive the highest energy and the highest vibration.

To call on the I Am presence is to acknowledge that you can unlock your codes and align with your divinity. You are divine and can align with the divinity because you have these codes. You are part of the Adam Kadmon race and can receive and align with the divine. This is the true meaning of the *Kaballah*—to teach you that you are a vessel to receive divine energy.

What does it mean to receive the transformational energy of *Eh'yeh asher Eh'yeh*? It is different from taking a cup that is filled with water; it is like taking a cup that is being transformed! You are not just a container holding the energy, but you yourself are transformed. You become one with the energy, and through the transformation, you are then able to participate with divinity. This is the true meaning of the *Kaballah*—to receive and transform. Accept that this is your birthright. The whole evolutionary development of the Adam Kadmon race is now moving in this direction.

SOUNDS FOR ALIGNMENT

You might ask why it has taken the human race so long to move toward awareness of the genetic codes. There have been many in your history who have understood these codes and how to use them. Now the whole Adamic race is taking the evolutionary step of focusing on an awareness of how to unlock these codes. It will not be necessary to keep the codes secret, because we are now in an extremely accelerated time. Many of you have incarnated now in order to use these codes to access higher energy states. When you go into a higher state, you can look down on your third-dimensional self and send love back to yourself.

Remember the famous story of your leader Moses, who had ascended to the highest energy. He returned, and around his face was the radiance of the higher energy field. You also will be able to heighten your radiance. You will be able to become more brilliant in your third-dimensional existence by entering into the states that we are describing.

We will work now with another sound that is very powerful, the sound of *Atah*[6] [sings]: *"Atah . . . Atah."* When you put yourself in alignment with the energy of *Atah*, you are truly beginning to vibrate in a way that will offer you protection through increased vibrational power. The purpose of using these sounds is to raise your own vibratory ratio. You are vibrating at a slow rate in the third dimension. In order to put yourself in congruence with the higher energies, you must raise your own frequency. The sounds of the Hebrew language can raise your vibration so that you can interface with the higher realms.

We will now use the sound of *Zohar*. This is a galactic sound found in many of your writings. It is a high-frequency sound associated with brilliance and white light, and it is used throughout the galaxy. It is one of the basic sounds in the Pleiadian language. If there is one word on Earth that is truly cosmic, it is *Zohar*. We will work with you now with the brilliance, with *Zohar* [sings]: *"Zohar . . . Zohar."*

The brilliance is light that is part of the Creator energy. If you are not able to increase your vibratory speed, then you will have an experience similar to looking at the Sun without the proper protection of sunglasses. You must work on raising your vibration. This is very important to do in your studying and in all aspects of your meditations. Prepare yourself so that you can vibrate at a higher speed. Then you will not have to worry about damaging yourself in any way [sings]: *"Chashmal*[7] *. . . Atah Gebur*[8] *. . . Le'olam Adonai*[9] *. . . Mechiye metim Atah."*[10]

Mechiye metim atah is a very powerful phrase used for the ascension energies and for the energies of transformation. Over and above what the words mean, this phrase is important for use in connection with transformations. When you are actually in the state in which you accept that you are prepared and ready to transform, then you may use the phrase *Mechiye metim atah*.

OPEN YOURSELF TO TRANSFORMATION

You must announce to yourself and to the I Am energies that you are prepared to transform. Part of the reception process involves being in a state in which you are open to transformation. It does not require years of preparation, nor do you need to go through major personality changes or learn elaborate new rituals. You are truly prepared when you feel open to receiving.

When you acknowledge that you are open to your transformation, then you are not holding on to any old self or to any tightness related to being a certain way. You then open to being with the way of the I Am presence. It is a giving up to receive—to receive the higher self, the I Am. This is the interactive energy. Totally giving up the ego is a difficult concept to understand. In this model, you give it up so that you can receive and transform.

If I want to call on my higher self, can I use the phrase "Eh'yeh asher Eh'yeh"?

That phrase will help you to align with your higher self. You understand that your higher self is always there; it is a matter of putting yourself into alignment with that energy. Yes, when you are accessing these phrases such as *Eh'yeh asher Eh'yeh*, you are unlocking the constraints you have on your normal ego functioning. The energy can come in because you have said the right code.

You must be careful when you use these codes, however. You want to do it in a state of meditation and comfort. You don't want to feel threatened in any way. You must do it in a place where you are able to open to the energy, and then use the codes very reverently.

Would the phrase be useful for healing?

First, you connect with the phrase. In terms of doing healing, I would use this phrase for only the highest connections. You can put yourself in a high state using this sound. Then when you wish to go on to healing, you can use other words that would be effective. Again, this is like unlocking the big door.

Would it be a good phrase to use to connect to your higher self as well as to spirit guides?

Yes, it is like a direct line, a direct contact. Use this phrase to receive the energy. You do not need to focus on any other intention. This is a total existential experience. Everything you need or want is contained in that phrase and in the interaction that will occur. Give yourself over to the phrase, and then have total confidence that whatever alignment you need to have at that point can occur through your concentration on this phrase.

Many of you are interested in doing other types of healing. The ultimate healing for yourself is the connecting. Then after that, all other healing can take place. All your energy channels will open up. You go to the highest connection first. There are other ways of healing without doing this, but we are working with you now on this level of energy. Be aware that you have made a connection and that you need to open to this connection. In some ways, it might not have been as strong as you wanted it to be, but on another level, it was as strong as you could tolerate. This connection is something that you have to work on. It will deepen as you give yourself over to your practice.

Notes:

1. One tradition associates Metatron with Enoch, who "walked with God" (Genesis 5:22) and who ascended to heaven and was changed from a human being into an angel. Because he had dedicated his life to piety, God took him up into the heavens where he was raised to the first rank of angels and turned into an angel himself. His name has been defined as the Angel of Presence.

2. The term "*merkava*" means God's throne-chariot and refers to the chariot of Ezekiel's vision. The *merkava's* goal is entry into the throne worlds. For more information, see Charles Ponce, *Kabbalah: An Introduction and Illumination for the World Today* (Wheaton, IL: Quest Books, 1973), 55.

3. This quotation is from the Hebrew prayer *K'dushah* (Holiness). The prayer reads:
   > Let us sanctify Your name throughout the world
   > As they sanctify it in the highest heavens.
   > As it is written by the hand of Your prophet,
   > "And they called one to the other and said,
   > Holy, holy, holy is the Lord of Hosts.
   > His glory fills all the Earth."

   Translation from Noah Golinkin, *Ayn Keloheynu* (New York: Shengold Publishers, 1989), 61.

4. Hurtak refers to this prayer as a mantra.

5. That is the supreme name of God, *Eh'yeh*, translated as I Am.

6. *Atah* is the Hebrew word for You, referring to the Creator. For example, the opening blessing in the *Amidah* prayer begins: "Blessed are You, O Lord." The *Amidah*, or Standing Prayer, plays an important role in Kaballistic meditation.

7. *Chashmal* is a mysterious term mentioned in Ezekiel's vision. It is a combination of two words, indicating speaking silence. What it means is the mental state through which one passes when one ascends from the level of speaking, whether verbally or mentally, to one of pure mental silence and sensitivity. It is only after this barrier is passed that one can observe a prophetic vision, as we see in the case of Ezekiel. According to Kaplan, when this state is reached, the ego is totally nullified and all sensation is hushed. For more information, see Ayreh Kaplan, *Meditation and the Bible* (York Beach, ME: Samuel Weiser, 1978), 41.

8. From the *Amidah*: "You, O Lord, are mighty forever."

9. "Forever Lord."

10. "You bestow life upon the departed." According to Hurtak, this is the code that is used to resurrect the dead.

CHAPTER 11

ON MERKAVA¹ TRAVEL

Archangel Metatron

I send down to you the golden-blue ray from the highest source to deep-en your spiritual connection to the energy of [sings]: "*Atah . . . Atah . . . Atah*." Let us speak about *merkava*, travel through *merkava*, and its relationship to your self and your highest self. We are now going to use the energy of the merkava vehicle while remaining in this realm. You can use it to heighten your presence in this dimension. Remember, you have heard that everything you need is right here with you; there is much energy and beauty on this plane. You can use the energy and the visualization of the *merkava* to enhance your presence now.

MERKAVA MEDITATION

Let us call on the merkava vehicle. Let your merkava vehicle descend around you as I call on the energy of the *merkava*. You will simply sit in the merkava vehicle where you are in your current place and feel any enhance-ments. As I sing the word merkava, you will call on your vehicle to surround you, and you may go into it [sings]: "*Merkava . . . merkava . . . merkava*."

Remember that the merkava vehicle is connected to your lightbody. As the astral² connection is through the silver cord, so the merkava vehicle is connect-ed by a cord of light that connects to your higher self and to your lightbody. Now, as your vehicle is around you, visualize the cord of light. If you are us-ing a pyramid, for example, the light cord will come from the top. As you are now in the *merkava*, visualize this light going up to your lightbody. I will sing in Hebrew the words for the light of the *merkava* that will accelerate and manifest your cord: "*Aur³ Ha Merkava . . . Aur Ha Merkava . . . Aur Ha Merkava*."

Now with this connection to the lightbody, feel a surge of light coming through the cord into your vehicle and filling you with the holy light from your lightbody. *"Aur Ha Kodesh . . . Aur Ha Kodesh."*[4] Now feel an enhancement, an acceleration, a healing, an opening. Focus on what it is you wish now for your present manifestation: *"Ruach Ha Kodesh . . . Ruach Ha Kodesh."*[5]

Step out of your merkava vehicle. Lift it up over you. Let the vehicle rise above you. Even though it is above you, it is still sending light down to you. You are being bathed in the light. The merkava vehicle will rise a little higher now . . . a little higher . . . still receiving light. Focus on the light coming down and sense that it is a holy light that is coming from a higher source, and you can receive it from your own *merkava* vehicle: *"Merkava . . . merkava . . . Aur Ha Kodesh."*

Your merkava vehicle rises higher and higher. It is returning to its source in your lightbody. You will still be able to connect with it.

Notes:

1. The Hebrew word *merkava* comes from the root *rakhav*: to ride, and it refers to a riding vehicle, or a chariot. In general, *merkava* refers to the complete system through which God "leaves his place" and reveals himself to those who are worthy. The idea of *maaseh merkava*, the workings of the *merkava*, refers to the setting up of a *merkava*, which is placing you in a state where you can attain a merkava vision. You can speak of making a chariot of light, or a merkava vehicle, through which you can ascend into other dimensions. Aryeh Kaplan, *Meditation and the Bible* (York Beach, ME: Samuel Weiser, 1978), 39.
2. The astral plane is the nonphysical level of reality considered to be where most humans go when they die.
3. *Aur* (also spelled *Or*) is the Hebrew word for light. In this context of *Aur Ha Merkava*, it refers to the light of the chariot, or merkava vehicle.
4. *Aur Ha Kodesh*: Hebrew for the holy light.
5. *Ruach Ha Kodesh*: the Hebrew words used to describe the state of enlightenment, which literally translates as "Holy Spirit." When God wishes to enlighten a person or convey a message to him, it is transmitted through the level of *Ruach*, or Spirit. Such a person is then said to have attained *Ruach Ha Kodesh*. Taken from Aryeh Kaplan, *Meditation and the Bible* (York Beach, ME: Samuel Weiser, 1978), 19.

CHAPTER 12

BEING A VESSEL OF LIGHT

Archangel Michael

We want to work intensely with you on bringing down more light energy. It is important that you continue accessing all the light power and light energy you can hold. It is a continuation and a participation process. Do not simply wait for the light to come to you, but rather encourage the light energy to come into your field.

You are a coparticipant in receiving the light energy. Do not think that just because you have been following this path—the path of light work, the path of the ascension—that the light will be around you. Of course you will have a certain baseline of light energy with you, but you will want to keep yourself in a vibration in which you have a feeling of continually making progress. This is extremely important.

Sometimes when you get in one spot, you may feel as if you are stuck. Although this is an illusion, it is very important for your own development that you have the feeling that you are continuing to grow and expand. The law of expansion is the law of the universe. Your guides and the angelic force are with you, continually trying to help you to set up circumstances in which you will have the opportunity to expand. You will feel and know that you are expanding. You will know that you are receiving more light because you will have the feeling of continuing to grow. This is so important!

LEARN TO BE A VESSEL

I ask you now to participate with us. We will be sending light energy down to you and I want you, as a coparticipant, to agree that there will be light strands around you. They are encircling your body field, your aura.

63

You can imagine it as a mummy wrapped up. Your aura is being encircled by this light energy [sings]: *"Aur Ha Kodesh . . . Aur Ha Kodesh."*[1] As the light is encircling you, you will notice the auric fields around your chakras[2] becoming brighter. This is a healing envelope of light energy that is opening up all levels of your energy fields so that you may access what you need to help yourself.

You may ask for what you need. You may ask for more than what you need! Do not fear that you are being greedy. Do not feel that you are being selfish. Your receiving light energy does not take away from anyone else's light energy. There is an endless source of this light. You are able to participate and receive it just by opening.

I want you now to focus on your heart chakra. Imagine that there is a discharge of energies and feelings that are unwanted but that you are holding on to. This discharge is flowing out very gently through your heart chakra. Your heart is feeling lighter and lighter as many feelings such as self-doubt, anger, depression, and worry begin to flow out of your heart chakra.

Be aware that you do not need to resolve your psychological or emotional issues in order to be a recipient of this light. Just understand and acknowledge that you can receive this kind of energy. As you receive this healing, it will help you to discharge things that you are ready to release. To be a coparticipant is to open yourself up and make yourself a vessel of light. Being a vessel of light requires that you know how to discharge energy.

In the heart of the *Kaballah* is the idea that you are receptors, or vessels. What does it mean to be a vessel? How do you learn to be a vessel? You learn to be a vessel by experiencing this process of spontaneously discharging and receiving. It is not something that has rigid steps. First, you acknowledge that you are a vessel. This is a genetic predisposition that you have; your body and your spirit are programmed to be vessels. Next, you allow the program to enact itself so that you are able to heighten yourself: *"Adon Olam*[3] *. . . Adon Olam."*

The path of making yourself a vessel means that you acknowledge the Master of the Universe, *Adon Olam.* You acknowledge the Father energy. You acknowledge the Creator-Son energy, Jesus-Sananda. You accept the path that is filled with their light. When you are on that path, you automatically align your spiritual energies so that you become deeper vessels.

Some have asked, "Where does the energy go when I receive it?" The energy goes into your whole auric self. It goes into your physical body. You are coming into alignment with your own soul light and soul energy.

Much of what you are receiving now is actually your soul light. This light is specially filtered so that you can access the light of your highest self. The esoteric writings only hint at this aspect of self. It is the "most-high" dimensional self. Many are not aware of its presence, but it is always behind the scenes.

YOU ARE A COCREATOR

This most-high self is the life force of your soul. There is a life force energy of your soul that some are beginning to seek an awareness and an understanding of. This highest soul life force is able to exist on the cocreator level. This life force is on the energy level that enables it to experience the Creator light, the highest light that you can experience or conceive of from this plane.

You are evolving now toward the cocreator energy.[4] Some are saying, "Well, how can we be cocreators? This only means we are on the same level as the Creator." In truth, your highest soul level is on the cocreator level. The Father's energy is above that. You cannot describe it. You can describe the lower Creator levels. There are many of the Father's guides and many of his hierarchical path workers who are assisting and making this road available for access. It is on this level that you will expand.

When you are preparing yourself for entering fifth-dimensional space, you must also understand that you are going to be on the level of cocreators. You must be pure of thought and pure of heart so you do not stain anything that you create. All must be created with the utmost love and the utmost respect.

I want you to envision a crown on your head. You are receiving a special light that is in the shape of a crown. This crown is the crown of the queen and king energy that will sit on your head tonight. There is a sparkling, iridescent, bluish-purple diamond that is in this crown, and it sits on your head now. Feel the energy, for you are as a king, you are as a queen. This is your birthright: *"Melek,[5] Gadol,[6] Mettrona—Shekhinah."*[7] Remember now that you are very open spiritually. You will be able to receive many things if you wish. Do not be afraid to ask for what you need, what you want, and even more. Ask now. If there is a reason why you should not receive what you request, let the reason come out now. Let us explore it with you so that you can remove the block. Let us now understand what is preventing you from receiving what you want.

Notes:

1. Holy light.
2. Centers of energy alignment that provide links among the spiritual, mental and biological systems of the human body.
3. Lord of the Universe: *Adon Olam* is also the name of a Hebrew song and prayer: "He is the Lord of the Universe who reigned before any being was created. He was, He is and He shall be in eternal splendor."
4. Becoming a cocreator is the ultimate fulfillment of your potential as part of the Source consciousness.
5. *Melek*: the Hebrew word for king. It is used in prayer to refer to God.
6. *Gadol*: the Hebrew word for great. It is also used as an adjective when describing God.
7. *Mettrona-Shekhinah* are two names for the divine presence. It is that aspect of the Goddess energy that is present on Earth.

CHAPTER 13

GENETIC THINKING AND MERKAVA

Archangel Metatron

We are happy to work with you on movement to higher dimensions. You can regard this lifetime as a preparation. You have been preparing more intensely during recent months and years to understand where you are in the space-time continuum, who you are, and what you need to do to survive. These are some of the requirements before you can open up to divine purpose.

Many of you have struggled to understand how you can be more useful on the planet. You are processing many different aspects of your existence, thought processes and genetic structures. Your thinking and beliefs are affecting your genetic programming. This is an idea that I have wanted to express—the concept of genetic thinking.

Meditations and work with belief systems affect your genetic structure. This means that you can conceive and visualize yourself as a being of light, a divine entity who is reaching into the higher realms. Your genetic structure will accommodate this projection, this image that you have focused on. You have heard many lectures about unlocking the genetic codes. Perhaps you have conceived that this is a complicated process. You might have even looked for a certain key or an equation.

It is a simplified matter to unlock genetic codes when your heart chakra is opened and properly in alignment. The alignment of your heart and other chakras can be accomplished through sounds. The very strong word *Kadosh* (holy) is an alignment word that opens your chakras. As you hear "*Kadosh*," then visualize yourself as a lightbeing and a divine entity who can travel through the dimensions, contacting guides and teachers. *Kadosh* can also work to lift your spirit out of your body and into another realm.

Unite with the Light Realm

Another important concept for the ascension is this: The body follows spirit. When your spirit reaches the other realm, then the body will follow. When you place spirit in this higher realm, your body follows. This is the ascension in a nutshell. There will be an evaporation of your physical presence. You must conceive that your physical presence can evaporate. This will be easy to accomplish because your spirit will be anchored on the other plane. You have mistakenly heard it said of the ascension that some are there and some are not, as if there were no preparation or participation. Now I am giving you the necessary instructions.

Focus now on your heart chakra as I enunciate the word *Kadosh* through the channel [sings]: "*Kadosh . . . Kadosh*." With the heart chakra now opening—and understand that even your major strides will be small compared to the openings you will have when you move into the spiritual realm—you may image yourself as a lightbeing. Imagine your body, mind, and soul together in a unification of light. Keep that picture in your mind.

The concept of transporting the lightbody is important. It is the theory of the *merkava*.[1] The *merkava* is the basis for the earlier work that has moved souls off the planet to higher realms. Be assured that there are those around who are specializing in the harvesting of the souls. This is a beautiful concept, and it is accurate in many ways. The *merkava* is based on the fact that you can direct your harvesting. It is a higher step to harvest yourself as opposed to being harvested. The *merkava* focuses on your active participation and direction. When you are directing, then you can go to the highest realm, because you have expressed your will. This is the divine will—the *Ratzon*, as it is referred to in Hebrew.

The divine will can be expressed by transporting yourself to and uniting with the light realm, or the *Aur Ha Kodesh*.[2] That is the divine will. All spiritual beings are in an evolutionary phase that is moving toward this light. The major concern for your development is not what is occurring on the planet in terms of Earth changes. You are here to experience a transformation to a higher realm. Your movement to light will have a positive effect on the planet and its overall energy fields. It will leave a wonderful trail of light behind.

Those who are of light can leave the planet. It is a beautiful transition that will electrify the energy field of the planet. It is important that you maintain this concept of light as often as possible throughout the day. I will be very direct. The light transformation, the ascension, is an option at any moment. It can be taken. The next two and a half years are especially critical, not only for the development of the planet, but also for your development. You are in the last lap. Focus entirely on your light presence. Picture yourself now as a lightbeing. Do not be afraid. You have the capability of doing this. Put yourself in a blue flame. I will incorporate a blue flame of light that will look like a fire. It is a special flame that will be with you now [sings]: *"Nefesh[3] Aur Ha Kodesh. Neshamah[4] Ha Kodesh.[5] Aur Ha Neshamah."*[6]

Do not hide your holy presence. You are also of the Kodesh light. You can announce this: "I am *Kodesh*." Focus on the blue flame. This is a good way to bring out the soul essence. It is also the concept of "bringing it down." You must remember that we are multidimensional. Space-time is difficult to describe in the third-dimensional realm.

The concept of the *merkava* can be applied to the blue flame. When you focus your energy on the blue flame, then it will move you. Put your spirit into the blue flame. When you look into the flame, then you can see me more directly. It is hard to look at a bright light without the proper protection. It is also hard to look at an angel directly. When we are encompassed by the blue flame, then you can experience our presence visually and emotionally.

The *merkava* is a method of connecting, movement, and transportation. I will be of service to you now and in the future—for your benefit and for the benefit you can provide to others.

Notes:

1. *Merkava* is the Hebrew word for chariot. It is often used in reference to riding the chariot from Ezekiel's vision. It is also used in describing a branch in *Kaballah* called "merkava mysticism."
2. *Aur Ha Kodesh*: Holy light.
3. The Hebrew word for animal soul, or lower soul. It represents the entire range of instincts. *Nefesh* is the raw vital energy needed to live on the planet.
4. The Hebrew word for divine soul. *Neshamah* is the highest grade of soul. It is often identified with the *sephira Binah* on the Tree of Life and with the *Shekhinah*.
5. The holy.
6. Light of the divine soul.

CHAPTER 14

ON HEALERS AND HEALING

Archangel Raphael

The healing you do transforms the healer as well as the person being healed. This is the basic message, the litmus test, of whether the healing you are doing is successful. It is when you as the healer feel transformed that both you and the one being healed can move into a higher realm together.

To be able to heal is a true gift. It is a sign that you have made progress in your soul journey. It is a sign that you are coming closer to your final liftoff from the planet. It is a sign that you are in harmony with the energies of Sananda. When you study the energy of his life, you know that it was for healing. When you study your beautiful *Kaballah*, then you understand that it teaches not only to receive, as many have correctly interpreted, but also to heal and to unify.

The ultimate healing you can do is to bring the self into unification with the greater, higher self and then into unification with the Father/Mother energy. This union refers to the subject of the *yihudim*,[1] the unifications. The *yihudim* are not to unify the Father/Mother energy. This is an incorrect interpretation, as the Father/Mother energy is already unified! It is your task to bring your soul and the souls of others into harmony with the Creator energy. This is the true unification. It is your task to help others. This task is so powerful that many who have achieved the unification energy have purposefully chosen the task of returning to work with others on Earth.

You will ask why. The answer is that healing is such a wonderful experience and that healing provides an energy that is particularly available here in your dimension. The unique healings that you can perform in your dimension are powerful, uplifting, and expansive. Many are incarnating just to be able to participate in this energy of healing.

THE MISSION IS HEALING

You are accurate in the perception that you are purifying yourself. You are accurate in thinking it requires the ability to harmonize and to release. As you are releasing, you make places within your lightbody to manifest energy in the third dimension and to receive the available healing light.

You are aware that there is a special healing light that can come into this dimension. I want you to think about this. Many of you are aware of your multidimensionality and wish to leave the planet and participate in other realms. We have provided you with many hours of lectures on the beauty of multidimensionality and on the beauty of existence in the other dimensions. But please do not forget how precious the energy is on Mother Earth. It is special to be healed, to be given light, to receive light, to participate in light, and expand yourself in the light on this planet. Stay grounded on the planet. This is the reason many are incarnating now. This is part of the cumulative effect of the preparations for the ascension: to be able to heal and be healed within the context you are now in on Earth—close to the ascension.

There is a special, powerful energy here now. Densities are present, and major changes are underway. Despite your incarnational struggles, focus on your willingness to be open. You are beautifying your soul by participating in the healing and by being a healer. This is a manifestation of your soul development, and it indicates that you are on the path you need to be on.

Many have asked us, "How do I know when I am on the path? How do I know what my mission is?" A healer never has to ask that question. The mission is healing and, ultimately, assisting in the planetary healing and transformation.

I wish to accelerate at a higher vibration than the light that you have been working with. I will be using the powerful word *Kadosh.* Know that when you are healing and when you are being healed, you are in the Holy Presence. Do the healings in the name of the light of the holiness, in the name of the energy some have described as the *Shekhinah.* The *Shekhinah* is an energy you can now experience in the third dimension. It is that side of the Creator Spirit that is especially available for you to participate in. It is not only open on the Shabbat[2]—telling people that the *Shekhinah* was available only on the *Shabbat* was a way of helping people to formalize access to that energy—but it is also available at all times for those who are pure in heart and pure in soul intention. Many have described it as a feminine energy. It is the same energy that Mother Mary was using in her lifetime. This energy first must be experienced as a healing light so that when you interface with the *Shekhinah* energy, you will have an experience of healing.

GREAT HEALINGS ARE AVAILABLE

What does it mean, my friends, to be healed? What does it mean to be prepared for the light? To be healed is, in essence, to be one and to bring those who are around you into that oneness so that they can experience it. You, as a healer, will use yourself as the tool to focus the energy from the *Shekhinah*. You are the artist and you are the brush so that the art can flow through your brush. You become a vessel [sings]: *"Shekhinah . . . Kadosh . . . Shekhinah . . . Kadosh, Kadosh."*

The abilities of healers are accelerating now. We are entering a period in which you will, as a healer, be able to perform masterful healings. As the one being healed, you can also have accelerated experiences. You will have these experiences not only when you are being healed by someone else but also when you, yourself, are performing the healing.

The healing experience is magnificent on both ends. In truth, it is best to work with those who want to be healed. This sounds simple, but many will be coming to you who are not ready to be healed. To be ready to be healed means to be willing to give up ego and self-centeredness. If you are working with someone who is still stuck, then you must help that person at the stuck place. Help him to release his self-centeredness. That could be a very powerful experience.

Finally, I ask you to use my name in your healings. Great healings are available if you make room for guides within yourself when you are doing the healings. You can help the healing by stepping aside to allow me or others to come through you. This is a gift you have, and it will increase your healing abilities. It will have a great benefit on your overall energy state. To step aside does not mean that you leave. To step aside means that you are allowing another's presence to be within you when you are doing the healing. This is a very artful process. I can work with you in a very effective way—whether it is through your hands or simply through your presence—if we work together.

OVERCOMING RESISTANCE

Remember that as an angelic force, we like to be called on. It increases our ability to be present in the third dimension. We will speak with you directly about how to help others in their healing, but the most important aspect of the ascension process is that you must engage in your own healing. Then as a manifestation of your light work, you will more effectively heal others.

More than anything else, an act of healing will convince people of the truth of the light. It will convince people that there is an ascension and that they can transform themselves. For many, until they experience healing, there will always be a doubt. Thus you can understand the relationships between yourself, your healing, and your role as a healer for others: Healing is the most effective way to transmit the light to others. Healing can be transmitted through light. We call this healing light *Aur Ha Kodesh . . . Aur Ha Kodesh*. Now bathe in the light of the *Aur Ha Kodesh*.

I must tell you that when you are healing others, you must first work with their resistance to being healed. You know from your work in psychology that there is always a resistance to being healed. There is a resistance even to the love that can be received at any given point. The resistance is there for many reasons, my beautiful ones, but the angels will send you love to help you overcome your resistance.

All of you are struck by the densities of this plane. Just by being in the density, there is some resistance. But we are talking about major resistance. When someone comes to you for healing, he or she is already in trouble and experiencing a darkness, already experiencing a closing down of the chakras and a closing down of the energy fields. The person is already desperate. You might first think that you can just open him up and send love and light and put him into alignment, and then he will be beautifully healed. In many cases, you will indeed be able to perfect a temporary healing and alignment by that method, but it is effecting a permanent transformation that we are working toward with you. It is this permanent transformation that you want to instill in others.

WORKING WITH LIGHT ENERGY

Now we will speak of how to go right to the resistance and heal it first, how to heal the reason the person does not want to change, and how to heal that dark spot within his or her physical manifestation that is creating the illness. Focus on the unloving energy within him or her. When you do the healings, whether they are verbal or whether you are transmitting light, you must first go and find that spot and work there.

Let us talk about techniques. You can go to that unloving part energetically, and you will find that there are aspects in the person's energy field that must be cleaned or picked out, like a gardener weeding. You must pick out those "weeds" first and then do the healing. Some have called that a clearing. This type of healing is more than just a clearing, however. This healing energetically creates a clearing in which you can also cleanse the auric field. Thus those you heal will be more prepared to accept the light energy you input.

When you are doing the healing, send a focus of light though the crown chakra using an overall white light. *Aur Ha Kodesh . . . Aur Ha Kodesh.* Then follow with the weeding technique, clapping and making sounds in order to help pull out the dark spots.

After the discharge of the dense energy constellation, it is important that you focus on the highest vibration possible. Perhaps you can view this as a surgeon sewing up stitches after surgery. After you have experienced the release of the density, or the block, then you may use the power words again: *"Aur Ha Kodesh."* In this energy state, complete the healing.

You have come into this incarnation to do this healing and to do this work. It is beautiful for you. Part of the reason for the confusion and the many problems that people are experiencing on the planet now is the magnificent amount of work that people are coming here to do. You can be involved in cleansing and repairing your own soul so that your aura does not have tears or rips, which are draining. After a healing, your aura will be totally sealed and in harmony. It will vibrate at a comfortably high rate, continuously self-generating and self-healing. *Baruch Hu . . . Baruch Hu.*[3]

The ability to heal others is deeply connected with your own ability to be self-healing. You will become a better healer as you open up to your own healing light. The time is short. Stay with your purpose and stay with the energy flow and exchange.

In conclusion, I want to emphasize the importance of discharging and weeding first, before you do the actual healing work. It is an important part of the healing, and you cannot separate one from the other.

Notes:

1. *Yihudim*: unifications; the enunciation of a simple statement prior to reciting a prayer. The intention of the person so doing is to bring about the unification of God and the *Shekhinah* (the feminine side of God). In *Kaballah* it is believed that human beings help to unify the two aspects of the Godhead through prayer.
2. *Shabbat* is the Jewish Sabbath, beginning on Friday evening. The Kaballist believes that the *Shekhinah* comes on *Shabbat* to be with people and to help make that day holy.
3. *Baruch Hu*: Hebrew, literally: "Blessed you," usually translated as "Blessed are You, oh Lord," referring to the Creator.

CHAPTER 15

ON FORGIVENESS

Quan Yin[1]

I am pleased that you are so attentive and eager for my message. I bring you a message of joy, love and peace. The task each of you has set out for yourselves in this lifetime is admirable. I want you to understand that you are undertaking major work in now. You are motivated to overcome blocks within yourselves so that you may grow and develop spiritually. The fact that you are struggling and facing those blocks is important to acknowledge. It is hopeful that many others like you are devoted to this path. Look at what is occurring in your lives. The problems you are having are part of the path you are walking.

THE EMOTIONAL BODY

Our leader Sananda-Jesus had a particular path that only he could walk. It served as a model for many to follow. You also have a unique path. Each soul has its own expression and its own uniqueness. There are aspects of your struggles that no one else can understand completely. Even though there are similarities with others, your path and struggles are still unique.

The subject at hand is forgiveness. Forgiveness ties in with many emotions. It ties in with compassion, empathy, anger, and love. Forgiveness is an opening to all of these emotions. Even jealousy, pain, and hurt can be tied strongly with forgiveness. One of the main tasks you have come to resolve centers on your emotional body. Most of you are fairly well-developed mentally and thus have the capabilities of grasping the concepts of higher dimensions and higher consciousness. Using these abilities, you can access your guides.

It is more difficult when it comes to the emotional body. This is no secret. You are evolving emotionally; in fact, the opportunity to work on emotional issues is one of the reasons people incarnate on Earth and one of reasons for coming back repeatedly. There is a long waiting list for incarnation on Earth now because Earth is one of the best places to work on emotions. You will not be confronted with disharmony and conflicts in the higher realms. You will be more in harmony with your emotions because you will be surrounded by others who are in harmony. In order to reach the higher planes, though, you must first resolve emotional issues. The biggest need for emotional growth resides in forgiveness.

The key to forgiveness—as to all growth—lies in the emotion of love; the necessary step of forgiveness requires loving. Be aware that loving contact with the other realms can accelerate the forgiveness process. It is difficult to do it entirely by yourself. You need assistance in forgiving. This is my message to you, my dear ones: Help is available from your guides and other entities surrounding you. They are willing to work with you on forgiveness.

Forgiveness can tie in on a multidimensional level with what has happened in a past life. An issue from a past life can create similar circumstances and the same emotions in this lifetime. You have returned, in part, to have that unresolved emotional experience from the past again. Forgiving means acknowledging the pain and releasing the tears. Forgiving means admitting that you loved the person who hurt you and that you might even still love that person now.

Problems begin when you remain caught up in criticizing the person who hurt you. True, that person did something to you that was harmful, and while you are still in that pain, it is easy to judge. Other people might say: "Don't judge; don't criticize!" They are still looking at forgiveness from a linear perspective. The question one really needs to ask is: "How can I judge or criticize when I do not have all of the information from the higher perspective?"[2] It is more difficult to understand actions when you are coming from a linear perspective. Acknowledge that you have judged the hurtful act. Make the judgment, and then don't dwell on it. Leave it. Not leaving it is where many of you are getting stuck.

GIVE YOURSELF PERMISSION TO TRANSFORM

I want to talk about light energy and healing your emotional body. Words alone are not enough to heal at times. There is a need for filling a void that was left empty. When someone hurts you, he or she takes part of your energy and robs your energy field. An actual hole appears in your aura. While that hole remains, you are missing a part of yourself. When that auric hole is repaired, forgiveness is completed.

I will give you sounds and transmit light to help repair aspects of your aura. Scan your body for places where you think there are holes. As you hear my sounds, I want you to bring light to the damaged part of your aura and feel a repair occurring. [Makes sounds.] The energy hole can now be repaired. Remember that sound can become light. Feel the vibrations entering your aura as healing sounds that become light. They can then integrate into you energetically. They can dislodge patterns and move blocks that could not be resolved previously.

Sound becomes light, light becomes healing, healing becomes forgiveness, and forgiveness becomes love. [More sounds.] Be aware of your aura. Feel faster vibrations within your aura. Imagine now that there is light in that part of you that needs to be repaired. The area where the hole was is now vibrating faster. It is vibrating in harmony with the whole aura. Imagine that my presence is within a room above you. I am standing over you with my palms open. Light is coming out of my palms throughout the room, pumping energy down into you, bringing healing light, gentle light, brilliant white light, and golden rays. Receive the light into your crown chakra.

You have a tremendous ability for self-healing. You have the ability for self-correction, energy release, and transformation. Know that what you are struggling with now is part of a transformation process. Tell yourself that you are ready to move on. "I give myself permission to transform." This is my affirmation for you now. I ask each of you to make this statement. Give yourselves permission to transform, then acknowledge that a new energy must enter. To transform, you need new input and a new energy. This energy is coming into you now. Process the energy now. Look it over and decide if you want to keep it.

I now change the light to blue. Blue represents spiritual energy, and it is spiritual energy that is the energy of connectedness to higher planes. The energy that is now coming down as I am standing above you is going into blue. We are filling your aura with blue light. This blue light makes your auras taller, more expansive. You expand when you are in your true aura. You are tall. [Makes sounds.]

My dear ones, I will leave you now with the feeling of being on an equal footing. You are resonating in your true selves. When you are in this realm, in this vibration, you are truly equal with the guides and angels working around you.

Notes:

1. Quan Yin: a female member of the spiritual hierarchy. In her previous Asian incarnation, she performed many acts of kindness and compassion and, because of this, is known as the Goddess of Mercy.
2. The higher perspective can include information from past lives or specific lessons that your higher self decided that you needed to learn in this lifetime.

B'NAI ELOHIM[1]

Sananda

W e will talk about the *B'nai Elohim* and belief systems, because that is such a powerful area of transformation. You need as much information as you can get about belief systems.

There are groups of people who believe that they have special answers and special dispensations. Therefore they believe that when they go to the higher place that some call heaven, they will be the sole occupants of that place. In truth, they will be. They will be in their own heaven. It will be as they had imagined it in many ways, and they will be with like-minded people. But that is not the only heaven; it is just their particular heaven.

At some point as they sit in their heaven, they will begin to understand that there are others who can begin to share in it. They will realize that there is no exclusiveness, that the gates of the higher dimensions are open to all. If they believe in exclusiveness, they are necessitating their return to the Earth plane. They will return in order to learn that lesson, because there is an aspect of karma involved when one is feeling exclusive and thus identified with a closed group.

Do not judge their belief systems; they have the need to mingle with such a group energy. That group energy is very important for their soul development. There is a purpose and a need for them to be in that group dynamic, whether it be a small or a large group.

YOUR ROLE IN SOUL DEVELOPMENT

It is important for you to understand the role of the soul and the role of belief systems in your future. Souls were not all created at the same time; it is a continual process. There are souls who are extremely old and have been around from the beginning of the Earth cycle of Adam Kadmon. Creation goes on continually in this universe and in other universes. New souls are coming in and coming of age in a place where they can come into awareness.

What is your role in this understanding? It relates to the important concept in the *Kaballah* called the *B'nai Elohim*, the sons of the *Elohim*.[2] You can see from your perspective that there is a progression of soul development. You are on a hierarchical ladder seeking a higher level of consciousness, a higher level of development for your soul. You will actually be able to achieve higher responsibility and authority in the universe.

There are many different planets. Do not think that the humans are at the lowest level of soul development. You are just used to the higher entities talking to you as if you are on the bottom. Believe me, there are those below you in the evolutionary cycle that many of you can help. Some of you have come from other planets, other sectors of the galaxy and even other galaxies. Despite the hardships and negativity here, you will be pleased to know that you came here because there are necessary lessons, knowledge, and skills on Earth. You will be able to take these lessons back with you when your soul returns to your home planet or home sector. There is much that you could take from this incarnation alone that will be helpful in teaching other souls.

The *B'nai Elohim* is a level of the hierarchy that is composed of souls who have gone through the ascension process and then progressed beyond the incarnational cycle of the planet. They are now able to go into the realm of higher authority. *B'nai Elohim* is translated as the "sons of the gods." This means that they are entering the level of authority where they could be involved in the creation of and the overseeing of a soul. You could be assigned a soul to follow for many lifetimes.

There is a place in the universe and beyond—not in the normal realms that you understand—where these souls are being created. The creation of a soul is like the birth of a baby. Special parenting and overseeing are required. One step in this process is the parenting. Another step is in the creation of the new souls. Just as there are parents on this Earth who create a baby—not a soul—so there are *B'nai Elohim* who work in harmony with others to create new souls. This is a monumental responsibility and not given lightly. When you reach the *B'nai Elohim* level, you are beginning to be on a master level where you can actually become part of the Christ energy yourself. You can become a Christ figure for a group of people. You can be a Christ figure in terms of redemption, transformation, and assistance to other groups. Remember, there are billions and billions of other planets in the universe, and there is much need for those who can serve in this role.

COSMIC DAY TRANSFORMATION

Let me speak of the progressions in terms of the cosmic day. There are aspects of the cosmic day that are like the eternity of this universe. There are different levels of eternity because there are different universes, and there are different days in the structure of the multi-universes that we know as the Great Plane.

In a sense, you are progressing on hierarchical levels, going from the Earth incarnation to the ascension to the master level to the *B'nai Elohim* level and then onward to work in the Christ light in other realms or on other planets. At the end of the cosmic day, you will have experienced a total transformation. Those who are on the highest level are able to sit next to the throne. When the total transformation occurs again, they are able to maintain their levels. From a soul perspective, you can see the benefits in continuing your hierarchical journey.

Now, many of you will say that you do not want to deal with the hierarchical level. It sounds like a linear progression. Yet when we are talking to you in the third dimension, this is the only way to describe it. There is a hierarchy of soul development in the universe. It comes back to belief systems. Your belief system is a reflection of your soul development. Those of you who are working for soul acceptance, unconditional love, and non-exclusivity are making a gigantic step forward.

Those of you who remain committed to beliefs in exclusivity and special dispensation because of your birthright can still be on a high path. Remember, it is important to the development of human children that they feel special. They need to understand that they have special places in the hierarchy. This is not necessarily a negative position. You must look at the holding of a belief in exclusivity as a lesson that must be learned, one that is appropriate to their special levels of need.

I understand that you want to feel special. You are special! All of you are special because you are dealing with your development, possibilities, and potential as a *B'nai Elohim*. I am pleased that you are grasping this concept and want to be trained and developed hierarchically. You can assume this responsibility and accept that in reality, you can be at the level of the Creator. This is extremely important.

YOU CAN BE A PARTICIPANT

Each soul is different. *Eh'yeh asher Eh'yeh*, I Am That I Am, means that you understand your uniqueness. Therefore, you do not have to be like others. Every soul that is created is unique, just as every snowflake is unique. The goal of a soul is to be its own uniqueness, to be its own self. "I Am That I Am" is a multilevel metaphysical statement. It is asserting your cohesion with the energy of the Creator. It is also asserting your own uniqueness and acknowledging that other souls are unique too.

The Father's directives are to allow all who can truly harmonize with the I Am That I Am energy to proceed on the hierarchical ladder to their destined development. This directive also acknowledges that the creation of souls is continual. Your soul did not exist from the beginning of time as you know it. Your soul came in at a later level. There are souls coming in now, and there will be souls coming in in the future. It is a continual process. You are reaching a point at which you too can participate in the birthing of new souls.

There is no such thing as the death of the soul. There is only the transformation and the development of the soul as it strives to be closer to the Throne of our Father. The higher you develop, the more you can be of service, and the more you are fostering the energy of the Creator and the Savior within you.

Notes:

1. *B'nai Elohim* are the Hebrew words for "the sons, or brotherhood," of the *Elohim*. *Elohim* literally means "gods." This is a curiously plural word, which also has been translated as gods or divine beings. In *Kaballah*, *Elohim* is God in his Creator aspect. The first words in Genesis are *Bereshith Bara Elohim*, which can be translated as: "In the beginning, *Elohim* created . . ." The English versions of the Bible translated this as: "In the beginning, God created . . ."
2. In this context, a small "g" is used.

CHAPTER 17

UNIVERSAL LOVE AND THE NULL ZONE

Gurhan[1]

You have been enthusiastic about the desire to enter other dimensional spaces. You have been very eager to learn how we exist in the sixth and seventh dimensions. You can comprehend our existence and learn to come to our space. Our space is filled with overwhelming light and love. We do not realize how loving it is until we leave our plane. Coming to Earth, we are reminded of earlier times when our system went through painful changes.

OPEN YOURSELVES TO RECEIVE LIGHT

The power of love is the opening gift to the other dimensions. You can connect to the universal love energy. This is an important concept. It is a feeling that you must open to within your heart chakra. An important genetic key is also unlocked when this chakra is opened. We are discussing opening to the universal love energy that emanates from the Creator Source and flows out through all universes.

You are like antennae by which you can pick up this love frequency. You must first learn to amplify the receptivity of your love antennae. We are not talking only about loving yourselves or even about loving the planet. These are, of course, very important aspects of loving, but we are speaking more galactically. We are talking about tuning in to the love energy that emanates from the galaxy. It is a special frequency. We will give you sounds that will help to amplify your receptivity.

All beings of light must learn to receive light. One of the ways you receive light is by sensitizing your antennae and your receptors. Pick up this energy, and receive it. Feel it. Listen to the sounds I send you and concentrate on your heart chakras. In the name of the Creator Source, we ask for your heart chakras to open. Become sensitive to the universal love frequency that is available throughout the planet. This love frequency is a connection with knowing and with the eternal interdimensional spiritual light. When you receive this frequency, then you know that you have eternal life.

The existence of this frequency is an important mental concept that you can incorporate into your thought systems. The attunement is a gift you have. When you attune to the frequency, then you can simultaneously give permission for the release of genetic blocks and open to space brothers and sisters of light.

THE UNIVERSAL LOVE FREQUENCY

We are aware of a deep connection between Earth and Creator energy. Overwhelming negativity, conflict, and destruction exist here, and many life forms on the planet are becoming extinct. But from a higher dimension, we can see that your planet is being slowly surrounded by a huge, loving energy. The seeds for this energy were planted by Sananda and others such as Abraham, Moses, and Buddha. This powerful energy has already surrounded Earth in her fifth-dimension shell.

You serve the planet by experiencing this love frequency. Starseeds have been taught to use the universal love frequency. It is required that a certain core group open and receive this frequency to help stabilize the energy and the shifts on the planet. Your acceptance and understanding of the shifts are important. You are all in special roles of light. Your sensitivity, thought processes, and belief systems have a tremendous effect on the planet. Your thoughts can affect the development of the electromagnetic planetary shift. What this means is that you are playing key roles. A few of you are actually playing pivotal roles in the energy of the planet.

Be aware that you are beings of light. This means that you can, in your natural state, transform, move throughout the galaxy, penetrate all levels, and return to the Creator. It is only as beings of light that you are allowed to enter the celestial hallways and gateways. When you resonate with the universal love energy, then you are on this path.

You have heard of the null zone. In truth, it would be fair to describe it as a purification zone. "Null zone," in your language, implies that nothing exists. When your electromagnetic fields are in alignment with your heart chakras and with the universal love energy, then you can vibrate on a level beyond conventional duality. You can move into a realm that is electromagnetically above positive and negative.

Going through a null zone will not affect you, because you will already be beyond duality. If you are not beyond duality, you will face several options: You could be cleansed, you could be washed out of this incarnation, or you could experience the null zone as a form of electric shock therapy and suffer temporary memory loss of who and what you are. Some have compared the null zone to the photon belt. The photon belt is a factor related to the null zone. Remember, when you contact the universal love energy, you will not be negatively affected by the null zone or the photon belt.

It is difficult for you to understand how, as electromagnetic beings, you can exist without duality. Your structure is based on duality; your heartbeat, pulse, and breathing are based on an in and out, one or two, active or rest cycle. How can you maintain your electromagnetic presence in a null zone? You can accomplish this because there will be a total electromagnetic shift in your thinking and feeling. It could be interpreted as a loss of ego because you will not differentiate yourselves from others. You see how important it is to maintain your group contacts with those who are of a similar nature.

Remember the basic saying: "I Am That I Am." Hold on to this very important assertion when you are going through the null zone. It is an instructional message that was given to Enoch. You will not lose your I Am That I Am. If you did lose it, then you could be thrown back into an incarnation cycle. Even the sounds of I Am That I Am are important and can be repeated as a mantra. It is a multipurpose expression. When you go through an electromagnetic shift, you can maintain your divine I-ness by using this expression.

THE MUSIC OF THE LIGHTS

You will then come to the many levels of colors. In your Hebrew texts, it is called the *Zohar*. In the galactic sense, *Zohar* represents the area of brilliance that occurs after you have left behind your duality of thought and your electromagnetic duality. You can then enter a new body of energy, a lightbody, that is of a higher frequency and is beyond duality. Then you will enter the brilliant, luminous light that some have called the supernal light.

You will also hear and see the music of the lights. When you enter the higher energy, sound and sight become merged. On a higher level, sound, sight, and feeling become merged into light-singing-love. When you use sounds, practice seeing the light at the same time. This is a powerful tool!

The light of the *Zohar* is a galactic light. This light leads to a series of Zo- har lights that go beyond the galactic presence to the universal presence. You can then enter into the brotherhood of galaxies. You are close to this light now in your developments.

There are light councils on Andromeda. Energies of light converge and shift and interact with the light-sound-feeling level. It is our gift to send this light to those of you who are open to it. When receiving this light, some will want to leave and go directly to Andromeda. Remember, we are your sister galaxy, a parallel galaxy in many ways. We understand. We are not judging what is occurring on your planet. When you move into this new electromagnetic unity, you will give up your judgments about what is occurring on your planet as well.

Notes:

1. Gurhan is a spiritual entity from the Andromeda galaxy in the seventh dimension.

CHAPTER 18

LIGHT WORK

Mary

I am happy to see that you are beginning to love yourselves more. Be assured that as you get more into this frame of mind toward yourselves, then you will be able to work with Earth. I know you realize that your mission is not only to work on yourselves and to remove blocks but that you are also here on a mission that has been called "light work" and that will help to heal Earth.

Many of you have been working so beautifully to send this energy to Earth. Many disasters have already been prevented or temporarily postponed because of the type of work you have been doing and the vibrations that people like you have been able to send into Earth.

The potential for devastation on Earth is very high right now. There are so many areas that are ready to explode politically, economically, and geologically, and that does not even include the energy that is coming in from outside your solar system, such as asteroids.

LOVE EARTH AS THY MOTHER

Yes, Earth is hurting. Yes, Earth is suffering. At the same time, as you are able to clear yourselves of some of your "imperfections," you will be better vessels of light. You will be better focused on helping Earth by sending love and taking care of Earth in any way you can. It could be as simple as picking up a piece of paper you see on the ground when you are on a walk. While doing something like that, say to Earth, "I do this because I love you." That little thought can be very powerful, especially in the minds of people like you who are becoming vessels and focuses of light. Part of what you can do is to focus that energy and give it back. I ask you now to send love to Mother Earth. She is holding up very well, carrying the many, many souls that are on the planet.

There are many who are destroying her in various ways, however. There are many fires going on now on the planet—fires you do not even know about. There are many pollutants in the oceans. The oceans are continuing to die at the same rapid pace as you hear about the forests. The expanse of clean and open ocean is diminishing very rapidly. The extent of the problem of the ozone hole you have heard so much about is being covered. You can work by sending your love to that space. Any little thing you do will be helpful.

Decide not to harm the planet. When you are cleaning up Earth, send this thought to Earth: "I do this because I love Earth." It is a very powerful statement. Part of Sananda's message is: "Love thy neighbor as thyself." The expanded message is: "Love Earth as thy mother." You take care of your mothers. Most of you would do so without thinking about it, and your mothers appreciate it when you take care of them. Caring for your Earth Mother, then, is one of the greatest gifts you can give her.

HEAL THE AREAS YOU LIVE IN

Many are concerned about Earth changes and catastrophes. I ask you to not focus too much on them; instead, focus on the healing. There is a great need for continued love to be sent to the California area. Many of you have been working to heal the fractures and the plates to ensure that there is no catastrophic change. Heal the area you are living in by sending light and love to those areas. Be vessels yourselves for galactic and cosmic energy. There is a need to focus the energy that is coming into Earth. One of the functions of humans—the Adam Kadmon, or the race of Adam— is to focus this energy of love on the planet.

Some will say, "There is so much destruction going on now. There is so much negativity. How can I make a difference?" You are able to make a difference because you are on a vibration that is healing. You are on a vibration of love and light. Is that not what you are about as lightworkers? As you are healing yourselves, you will better be able to send that energy to Earth and to others.

I am proud that you have remained so devoted to this path. Continue to cleanse yourselves so that you can be who you are, and focus the energy on Earth. It is true that Earth will take care of herself. It is true that there have been many changes on Earth before. But never before has there been so much love directed toward Earth. Even as those who are destroying it seem to be doing it with greater intensity, those who are loving her are also focusing a new energy on Earth. There will be many dramatic changes. In past catastrophes, there have been healings and the saving of lives during major changes.

So my friends, I bid you a deep love. I bid you a deep respect for the path you are following. Do not underestimate the effect you are having on the overall planet. This love and light you pass on will affect your daily lives in human relationships. Begin by projecting love and light to those in your thoughts and to those with whom you interact. It is truly amazing how powerful the projection is when you send that energy. Think about it as a special gift of the race of Adam. Remember how powerful you can be just by thinking and by projecting your feelings of love.

Do not be too concerned when you hear of something negative occurring. You will simply send love to that area with your thoughts too. Please, as you go through your week, see if there is something each of you, in particular, can do for Earth. Do you have any concerns about the planet you wish to discuss tonight?

EARTH CHANGES

In recent weeks, there have been lots of storms in the U.S. Is this Earth releasing?

The magnetic currents around Earth have changed because of the thinning ozone layer, and that is creating different electromagnetic patterns that are affecting the winds. That is part of what is happening. The ozone hole is also changing the ocean temperature. Intense energy is now being received. A lot of it is going into electromagnetic vibrations of Earth. The thinning of the ozone layer is the most dangerous change that is occurring. The larger opening is affecting the electromagnetic field of Earth.

The ozone hole continues to get larger?

There is nothing that has been done to stop it. You are not hearing about the ozone hole in your media. What is released is in false pictures, like, "It is not as bad as we thought. There is no observable damage." It is the same as people saying there is no such thing as global warming. The issue is not so much whether this or that is occurring; the issue is that Earth is rapidly changing in an extremely short period of time. What will happen next is totally unpredictable from your standpoint.

It can't be the way it was?

It is no longer the way it was. About the storms, I can specifically say that the unpredictable weather patterns will continue.

Can we affect the ozone hole with our thinking?

The remaining ozone could become more effective in shielding the radiation. That would be a good healing energy to send to Earth. That which is left would then truly be more effective.

The other perspective about the ozone hole, though, is that now that the hole is larger, other galactic energy is free to enter. There isn't always just a downside to things. The Earth changes have been so intense that extraterrestrial and extragalactic forces have been required to become involved in the process, which is also a positive aspect.

CHAPTER 19

ADAM KADMON AND ZOHAR LIGHT

Archangel Metatron

There is a combined effort on many levels to bring Earth and you to the fifth dimension. This effort is coordinated by our beloved Sananda who is the master, or the captain if you will, of Earth's transition to her rightful place. He also oversees the transition of many souls like yourselves to higher levels. We—and many—acknowledge that Sananda is the leader and coordinator of this effort. That includes those from extradimensional or extraterrestrial (ET) realms. Any being who is coming from an ET realm and who is working for the ascension will acknowledge that the divine leader of this plan is Sananda. His cooperation and his special information with the Creator Source provide the data and guidance for us to assist you. It is important to work with the ascension codes and links. You are waiting to be processed and also wanting to open wider to this information. You want to open up to what is called the Zohar light.

The Zohar light is a special light that goes from one end of the universe to the other. This light, like all light, travels infinitely, but the Zohar light is a powerful light that goes not only through the universe but is linked directly to the Creator Source. This is a strand of light that exists throughout the whole universe and goes back to the Creator. Consider the Zohar light as being that kind of light that goes back to the beginning of creation. Can you imagine a strand of light that goes back to the moment of creation and travels from there directly to the Creator? You all know the statement, "And God said, Let there be light: and there was light."1 This strand of light is connected through the abyss of nothingness to the Creator. This special brilliant light is also invisible to most people, but it is a light that can be called on. It is a light that can be seen through the eyes of Adam Kadmon, or the primordial man.

THE PERFECT BEING

The primordial man is the first prototype that was created from which all souls of the human species emanated. There are soul families, and you are a part of a soul family. There is also one huge soul family that is a part of the Adam Kadmon source. You all belong to this, so all of your souls are linked to this. Now when you pass through the stargate, you can go to other species. You are not Adam Kadmon for the rest of your soul existence. You have committed a great deal of effort to the Adam Kadmon species. You can begin now to go to other species and other experiences in the galaxy.

The prototype of the Adam Kadmon is powerful, and it has been shifted and changed. It has been linked to other systems. Adam Kadmon has special codes to see the Zohar light. When you see this infinite light, you become brilliant yourself, and your eyes become brilliant. Once you have seen and experienced this Zohar light, your eyes will always be different. Your eyes will never be the same. But these eyes that you see with now are closed—they are not open eyes. The eye I speak of is the inner eye, your inner knowing eye. The opening of the Zohar light can begin with the expression, "Holy, Holy, Holy is the Lord of Hosts": *Kadosh, Kadosh, Kadosh Adonai Tzevaoth*. [Repeats several times.] Let the sounds of these words release the clouds around your eyes so that you can begin to hear my instructions and experience the Zohar light. [Repeats the above again.]

Please envision Adam standing in the Garden of Eden, for in the Garden of Eden, Adam could see the Creator Light. This first Adam is in your memory and in your cellular structure. The first Adam was also what you would consider to be a hermaphrodite. The first prototype was a man and woman together. It may be difficult for you to conceive of this, but it was neither an apparition nor anything that was bizarre. It was a perfect being that was able to reproduce from one as one being. But you know that it was made to be two as well. Go back in meditation to Adam—in whose body you are. You are in his/her mind, and you can see through his/her eyes. When Adam looks outward, he/she does not know the difference between the Zohar light and other light. For it is so high in vibration that he/she does not know how high he/she is. He/she does not know the vibration level he/she is on. From your standpoint, this reflects the sin of

Adam. For he/she knew not what he/she was. When he/she stepped out of the curtain surrounding the garden, he saw the difference. But once you see the difference, you cannot go to not knowing the difference. This is the "original" sin as you have described it.

THE PURSUIT OF HARMONY AND LIGHT

Now you are helping to rebuild this perfected state of consciousness through your work as an ascending master. You now see the difference between the light and the not-light. You would only like to see the light. You are not interested in the darkness any more. You are not interested in duality. Some ask, "How can the fifth dimension be described?" The fifth dimension is a place where there is no duality. So you see, when you are with the mind of Adam, you begin to re-experience your desires to be without duality.

You have seen duality and experienced duality on the third dimension. Most of you are tired of duality. You wish to be only of harmony and light. It is because you have experienced duality that you are now going to be clear about being only in the harmony. For like Adam, you stepped out of the garden, and now when you step back in—the garden being in the fifth dimension—you will experience joy and the ecstasy of being there. That is what going to the fifth dimension is about. That is what the higher consciousness is about. You have earned it. You are going to this state because of what you have prepared and what you have experienced. So everything you have experienced now in duality becomes valuable because you will appreciate and choose the harmony of the life of the fifth dimension.

So you see, Adam stepped out of the fifth dimension but did not know how to return. He/she did not know how to deal with the polarity. Perhaps that is where many of you have become stuck—stuck on how to deal with the polarities that are here. It is easy to say that you would like to be in the fifth dimension where there is unity, and overcoming duality will assist you in this. You can also say, "I am ready to leave duality." Maybe that will make it easier for you when you understand that you are tired of the duality.

Jesus Christ said that he would send us the Holy Spirit and then we could become One, and that the Holy Spirit could reconcile the opposites. I would like for you to explain that more.

Well, the Holy Spirit is what Archangel Michael called *Ruach Ha Kodesh*, which is the enlightened spirit. It is that part of our consciousness that is missing, and it is that part of your higher lightbody that comes down to you. When it comes into you, you see that all is One, but it is the Holy

One. We call it the Holy Spirit, because you begin to see the holiness of the unity. This is very important, because you must understand that this holiness is a unity. Adam, as the prototype, did not understand that he was in a holy state. When he lost that state, then he saw the duality. He looked back and knew that that was a holy state, or at least he had some perception of that. But he was already stuck.

Now a way out is provided, and in many respects, it is through the Holy Spirit. It is by making your spirit whole and holy again by acknowledging that the duality is overcome through the Holy Spirit. The Holy Spirit is the part of you that is your lightbody. It must descend on you so that you can experience this. This is the part of the unification that you are going through in terms of bringing your lightbody in unity with yourself.

DUALITY AND POLARITY

When talking about this integration of a lightbody—that two thirds of the lightbody would integrate—it seems to me that what holds us from unification at this point in our evolution is merely our thoughts.

It is your thoughts of duality. I would say to you that you do not realize how deeply engrained the duality and the polarity thinking is within you. When we speak of the Holy Spirit, it is of the understanding and thought that "I Am One." The Creator is One; you are One with the Creator. But there is much confusion, because you think, "Well, what happens to me if I am unified? Where is David? Where is Gudrun? Is there a loss of self?" You were trained in duality, and it started from the first day you were born.

This is one of the beauties of group consciousness that the Arcturians teach you. They wish to teach you that their/your merging into a group is positive and is not giving up identity. The Hebrew prayer *Shema* begins with: God is One. That is why we are saying: "I am One with God." So begin to re-assert the unity thinking in your prayers. "I am One with the Holy Spirit."

The Holy Spirit is that part of self that is already in contact with the unification energy. If I make your spirit holy, then I give you the unity thinking. I give you the ability to go back into the Garden of Eden and again experience unity. You will appreciate it now because you have seen the duality and the polarity. Now, some say that duality and polarity is the law of the universe. I say that it is the law of the third dimension. There is a higher unification than the polarity that you experience here. There is a higher wisdom, and it cannot always be seen from the perspective of the third dimension. But if you come to the fifth dimension, then you will begin to see this perspective.

If Adam was a hermaphrodite, what was Eve then? Complete? Looking alike? Was there no polarity happening, then, between the male and the female?

When Adam broke, shall we say, the contact with the fifth dimension, then the hermaphrodite could no longer be there. There then needed to be the polarity. Going from the fifth dimension to the third dimension is breaking into polarity. Therefore it became necessary to split Adam. So you could say that Eve was made from Adam. In essence, the soul was divided. Half of his soul became her, and that was the beginning of the polarity.

What necessitated the creation of Eve?

The actuality of that break with the fifth dimension occurred before Eve was created. Your Bible reflects that duality happened after Eve was created and implies that perhaps Eve was helping to create that. I would propose to you that Adam was a unity as a hermaphrodite. He was a kind of prototype. It was the breaking of his/her connection with the fifth dimension that led to the polarity of man and woman. To say that it was the woman who somehow deceived or made the man go wayward is an interesting but inaccurate spin on that story.

There are species in the galaxy that are hermaphroditic—Earth was not the only case. There are stories of hermaphrodites in your history. Can you imagine if all were hermaphrodites on this planet? Would you be male or female? You know that you all have both male and female within you now, but you all are predominately one or the other. This is not a story you would hear in the regular sermons on Sundays about the development of Adam.

But I ask you, why is the woman put in the light that she is in the Old Testament? Why is the woman seen as causing the man to eat the fruit?

Those who wrote that were from a male-dominated culture. They were trying to fight against the goddesses who were being worshipped by pagans. You see, the Adam prototype contains all of the souls that were the first source for all humans. You could have come from another species to this planet. All who come onto this planet somehow have to pass through the Adam prototype to receive the codes on how to become a perfected Earth human.

The Point of Separation

It is not androgynous then? It is not in balance?

Why would it not be in balance? Do you think the word androgynous refers to it being male and female together in your language?

Yes.

Hermaphrodite is also male and female. Both hermaphrodite and androgynous energies are totally in balance. Now, would an androgyne or hermaphrodite look more like a man than a woman? How would you describe it? You know that even though you are a woman, you have male traits. So now you can see where this comes from. Why do you have both traits? Why not pure male and pure female? This is why this whole issue seems difficult to resolve on the third dimension.

The issue of homosexuality seems like a big joke from this higher perspective. There is no sin involved in homosexuality. There is no problem because the people are experiencing part of the hermaphroditic energy. It is much more of a sin to kill and murder or to destroy the planet than it is to be loving. So being unloving is the sin rather than engaging in one sexual practice or another. When you understand the hermaphroditic origins, perhaps you may have a different perspective on homosexuality. It was the issue of turning away from the fifth dimension that led to the separation. It became imperative that when there was that separation, the male and female had to be divided in a manifested way. That is, it had to be physically manifested, and this is how it was separated.

But the separation was not exclusive to the turning away from the fifth dimension.

It was the turning away from the fifth dimension that started it and necessitated it.

Does that hold true as you go up the dimensions?

That is right.

I'm looking for clarification. The point of separation was separation from all aspects of multidimensionality, from the fifth throughout the other higher dimensions. Is that right?

Particularly the separation from the fifth to the third dimension. The creation of this prototype occurred at a higher level. The creation of the prototype did not happen on the third dimension. The creation happened at a higher level. As the duality became apparent, it then manifested as the separation of the sexes.

EVOLUTION OF THE HUMAN PROTOTYPE

Chronologically in the planetary cycles, when did this occur?

I am going to explain to you that, as this prototype, you were brought to Earth. This prototype design was brought to the planet by an external force. From your perspective, this would be somewhere between 150,000 and 200,000 years ago.

Isn't there evidence that man existed before that time?

Yes, there is.

Are you referring to the still-open link or to the true identity of the Neanderthal and Cro-Magnon type?

We are speaking about that. This is new information that we are sharing. What we are talking about with you has not been explained in detail. Some of you believe in the evolution of man. There was a point at which the Neanderthal man shifted to the Cro-Magnon man and eventually shifted to your present human form. But this was all going on before this was interlinked. You are interlinked in this chain. This is a very controversial subject when you think about how you got introduced into this link on Earth. What was the missing link?

Were there some dark forces that tampered with the pattern of the DNA?

I would say yes. There was tampering with that DNA, and now there are within your DNA codes some densities that were not to be there.

My question dovetails on what you just said. I am trying to place this with the influence of the Anunnaki. Is there a relationship to when this prototype developed and when they came in with their influence?

There is a connection. I would say that there are many who wanted to use your species for their purposes. There has always been a vulnerability in your species to misuse by others. There was tampering, as was suggested. How does all of this to affect you? You have different problems in integrating things because of this tampering. You have problems in integrating violence and hate. You see a lot of hate and destruction and desecration of the environment. These are all patterns within you that have been brought down to you. They have been brought to you. You must somehow come to terms with them and accept them and put them into balance and into their place so that you can transcend them.

You must accept them, but you do not need to act on them. There are people on your planet who act on them without showing any type of remorse or self-control. This is a battle within yourselves to overcome these negative forces. I would say that knowing this part of your history means that you can realize that there are parts of yourselves that have to be put in their place; these are parts of yourselves that you can acknowledge but not act on. Some of you have called it the primitive self. Some have called it other things. All is not beauty and harmony within the historical context of your development as a species.

Your Form in the Fifth Dimension

Will Mother Earth stop accepting people from the dark side?

When she is ready to go into the fifth dimension, the dark side will not be able to enter into Mother Earth. Believe me, there is always the desire to use this. Why was the dark side allowed to come and influence some of this development? I think it has to do with the fact that Earth is a free zone, and therefore the dark forces could enter the Earth realm.

We are especially interested in exploring your hermaphroditic origins. We are interested in exploring with you how you conceive of yourself in terms of male or female when you go into the fifth dimension. You are going to have to reunite yourselves into that hermaphrodite form.

Will it even be a question at that point?

A question of whether you can do this? No. It will not be a consideration for you individually as you enter the fifth dimension. I think you will just do it. One of the things you might ask, however, is how do you overcome duality? Now, you might ask, "Am I going to become male or female? How do I pass through the stargate?"

That might be the moment of hesitation.

Well, you could back out of going to the fifth dimension. This is something that has not been explored very much in the recent literature about the fifth dimension. I don't think you are going to back out of it. I think that perhaps it is a duality that you have not overcome. How do you integrate? It is an integration that you can prepare yourself for. There needs to be more understanding about this sexual process on this planet now, because there is a lot of hatred. There has been a lot of criticism about sexuality. Sexuality is an expression of the hermaphroditic nature that is the basis of your prototypes. Now, I am not encouraging you to act out and become hermaphrodites. Do not misunderstand me on that. I am trying to help you to reach this understanding.

It has not been something we have thought about.

There are several races in the star systems and in the fifth dimension that are hermaphroditic. There are even some who have been in the third dimension who have been able to maintain the hermaphroditic species.

I would say that Adam Kadmon was brought here. Once the vision of the fifth dimension was broken, he became involved just like everyone else.

INTERACTIONS AMONG DIMENSIONS

So Adam Kadmon was actually brought to Earth and then did what species do, which is marry with the other evolving species that were here? Is this correct? Is the fifth dimension a place like heaven?

The fifth dimension is such a place, but it is an overlapping place, so you would have a hard time envisioning this. The third, the fourth, and the fifth dimensions are layers. You could say that the fifth is right "here." Where is here? It is in another level. The dimensions are layered. They are layered in a way that you cannot see them, and there is interaction between the dimensions. There is an interaction of the third dimension with the fifth dimension, for example: "as above, so below."[2] So there are interactions. This is why the Arcturians and other fifth-dimensional beings are concerned and want to work with you.

Certainly the actions of the third dimension do have reverberations around all the dimensions. It is not an isolated state. So, for example, what is going on in the South will affect what is going on in the North. You cannot avoid it. I think the Adam prototype, the hermaphrodite, was a very powerful prototype. We had recommended at one point that the channel refer to it as Adam-Eve Kadmon. It is important to make contact with the Zohar light.

Can we still do it?

Yes, we can still do it, and I will provide directions for that. It is almost like asking, "Is God male or female?" How are you going to answer that? I want you to go back in time to this prototype that is Adam-Eve Kadmon. We can use the name Adam-Eve for this group now. You have access to this prototype, because it is in your DNA structure. It is within your cellular structure. [Tones.] *"Zohar."* I call on the Zohar light. It is the light from the beginning of the universe and from the beginning of the big bang. It is a stream of light that was connected to the spot that began this cycle of the universe. Know that this spot has a thin line of light that was at the beginning, and it is still here. A thin radiant light is available in all directions in your third-eye consciousness. [Tones.] *Zohar.* Let the Zohar light shine through the eyes of Adam-Eve Kadmon. Let it be received, and let the stream of brilliant light come into your consciousness. It is this light that the Creator communicates to us.

Those of higher vibration, like Sananda, can intercept that light and make a meaningful interpretation of that light to all. That is the true role of Sananda-Jesus: that he can be the interpreter of that light. It is a brilliant, bold, magnificent, and powerful light. Connect to that Zohar light now. You can be connected to the beginning of Creation. You are looking through the Adam-Eve Kadmon eyes. As higher beings, you can experience this light as a burst. It is as powerful as the first rays of dawn. This light can be used and transmitted to others by sound and by thought. The most powerful way of transmitting light is through thought.

Notes:

1. Holy Bible, Genesis 1:3. Hebrew, from the Torah: *vayo'mer 'Elohim yehiy' aur vayehiy 'aur.*
2. This phrase is an adaptation of the following text: "That which is Below corresponds to that which is Above, and that which is Above corresponds to that which is Below, in the accomplishment of the Miracle of One Thing." Hermes Trismegistus, *The Emerald Tablet*, 2:1.

CHAPTER 20

UNIFICATION

Sananda

I am here to give you messages about unity and the sacred codes. Unification will occur. You must be convinced of this at all levels. There is a process that is now occurring throughout the third dimension. Some of it is causing major separations and disharmonies, but there are also major unifications that are coming about. The unifications are what you need to focus your energy on. The Sacred Triangle is a unification, and there are other unifications at different levels.

When you describe these unifications, you must also refer to codes. There are genetic codes, there are spiritual codes, and there are ascension codes all within your structure. In fact, the Sacred Triangle is a new code that is emerging in this dimension. It is a code that will gather people together—a code that will be used by others to expand and create a corridor to bridge the third and fifth dimensions. The third and fifth dimensions are closer together now, and you and others are continuing to build bridges from where you are to the fifth dimension.

RELEASE

Each bridge and each corridor that you connect with is bringing the fifth-dimensional light that much closer to the third realm. The importance of this is tied into unification. What is happening is a unification that is going to occur with the third dimension and the fifth dimension. That moment of unification will be the ascension. From one perspective, that moment will last only for a brief moment. From another

103

perspective, for those like yourselves, it will last as long as you need to come into the proper energy to move to the fifth dimension.

This brings the concept of the relativity of time to the forefront. Those on the "outside" who are not into the unification and not into light work will see but a flicker and may not even see you go. You who are in this process will have the time to assimilate and move. It will be a brief moment. You will acknowledge that you are ready to ascend, and then you will go through a wonderful tunnel or a wonderful corridor to the other dimension. I assure you that the traveling and the moving to the other realm are going to be pleasurable. It will be one of the highlights of your experience as a soul traveler. Many of you have come to Earth at this time to experience this wonderful transition. It is a powerful transition, and it will be done with consciousness.

Many of you are coming here to accomplish some wonderful releasing. You know the importance of releasing attachments, negativity, conflicts, and also the completion of your karmic debts. Know of the power of grace. You will have an opportunity to accelerate your release and your karmic process. You can be very accelerated; you can move very quickly toward releasing. *Releasing karma is not a matter of time. It is a matter of intent.* It is a matter of consciousness. It is a matter of beauty and acceptance. I know that you are ready to release and prepare.

Codes of the Sacred Triangle

Let me speak about the codes. Each side of the Sacred Triangle has certain codes. I will speak of the codes of the Father/Mother energy. [Sings]: "*Adonai.*" The code for the unification and mastery of the third dimension is in the realm of *Adonai*, the Lord. Open this side of the Sacred Triangle for yourself. Be in harmony with the dominion and with the Father/Mother energy when you move to the creation and bring in *Elohim. Adonai Elohim.*

It is the creation that is the source of the light. You must connect with the creation, for your soul comes from the creation. You were unified and you separated as souls, and now you come back together in unity. Each side of the Sacred Triangle provides an aspect and a coming together of these soul energies. Within you, my brothers and sisters, is the code of life, the code of ascension, and the code of your higher selves.

You know that the sacred code is "I Am that I Am." It is the sacred name of the Lord. It is the name that was brought forth for you to understand that it is part of you. When you hear the code, "I Am that I Am," you connect with that aspect of the Father/Mother energy.

Hear these words and allow an energy light to burst up your spine and your crown chakra. Go to a high light, higher place, as high as you can go. *Eh'yeh asher Eh'yeh! Eh'yeh asher Eh'yeh!*

As you go up, feel the wonderful connections you can make! Know that many ascended masters are available to you, as well as the Arcturians, the Pleiadians, and other extraterrestrial masters. There is life throughout this galaxy. There is life throughout this universe. There are other dimensions, and other beings exist in interdimensional areas. It is time that Earth humans understand the existence of these dimensions.

You are going to connect with the dimensions so that you can graduate and move to a higher-dimensional realm. It is more exciting and expansive than you can imagine. You are confined to the third dimension. It is a beautiful place, but it is filled with many contradictions and many densities. How beautiful it is to come to this light and this opening. Rest assured that there is a beautiful opening that all of you are moving toward. Some say the opening is once every 2,000 years. Some say it is every 12,000 years.

The opening that is coming is so expansive that many of you have reincarnated at this time just to be here for it. Do not be sidetracked. Do not forget your mission—a mission of unification. Use the codes for internally, psychically opening your auras and the energy levels around your bodies. Use the codes to remind yourselves that you are going to just be focusing on the codes and the mission. Do not focus on the other densities.

Holy, holy, holy is the Lord of Hosts. You could also say, "Sacred, sacred, sacred is the Lord of Hosts." Holy is his place. Sacred is his place. "Where is the Lord; where is *Adonai Elohim*; where is YHVH?" It is where you make a place for his/her sacredness. That is the unification you provide. Your job is to bring this connection. *Kadosh, Kadosh, Kadosh Adonai Tzevaoth!*

A SACRED PLACE

I call on you to make this place sacred. Make this gathering holy. You are unifying the dimensions. That is what sacred places are. They provide and they manifest the unification of the fifth and the third dimensions. It is our Father's/Mother's will for you to evolve to the higher realm, and messengers and masters are sent to stimulate you to this now. There is a necessity for more sacred and holy places, whether it is the Sacred Triangle Healing Center, a church, a synagogue, a holy place on a mountain, in your home, or whether it is in you.

You can indeed become the holy man or holy woman, for wherever you are is a manifestation of the unification of the third and the fifth dimensions. Suddenly you become lighter, and the codes remind you—you know that you need to be reminded over and over again. You know that it is a difficult challenge to come through all that you have come through in this lifetime. It is difficult to even come to this level of awareness and this level of spiritual development. Look what you had to go through as a child. Look at the work you have to do now just to come to this place. Yet you have made it. You have come here as part of your fulfillment. You have many alternatives. You can be a holy man or holy woman. You can make a place sacred and holy. This includes making corridors. You can work together and make structures that are holy.

Where is *Adonai's* place? Where does *Adonai* reside? What many say is that you cannot speak of or describe him/her, yet you can experience him/her. This experience comes to you as holiness and as sacredness. There are codes to remind you of this. This is what we are talking about when we refer to planetary healing and planetary transformation. Go from the holy of the self to the holy of the community to the holy of the planet.

I say a blessing for Mother Earth. The sacred and golden ring of ascension remains around Mother Earth. It is a ring of light that is a manifestation of the interaction between the third and fifth dimensions. It is a ring of light that you have helped to create. Just as you have an aura, so also Earth has an aura. Just as you now are focusing on golden light around your head, so does the Earth.

You can contribute to the sacredness of this. Look at the work of the Arcturians and the designation of the Sacred Triangle. Notice the term "sacred" again. It could also be called the Holy Triangle. The Sacred Triangle acknowledges the unification of Earth energies with the fifth-dimensional energies of our galaxy.

THE FIRST LIGHT

It is time for people to understand that you are part of a galactic family of beings. Why has this been hidden for so long? Why do so many people have difficulty accepting their galactic heritage? It is denser thinking and ego thinking. People used to think that Earth was the center of the universe. Remember the absurdity of that view. Unification does not diminish you; it enhances you.

You become holy spirits. A holy spirit is an enlightened spirit. Enlightenment—you have tried for enlightenment in many lifetimes. You are now enlightened. There is no question about it. I look at everyone's auras, and I see smiling light. I see happiness. I see spiritual acknowledgment. The way to enlightenment is through spiritual acknowledgment. The way to enlightenment is through fulfillment of mission. The fulfillment of mission has to do with unification and acknowledging the codes.

The codes that are presented to you have wonderfully come before you as a mission and light of the Sacred, Holy Triangle. *Ruach Ha Kodesh*—the Holy Spirit. Move from the holiness of you and the holiness of a place to the holiness of a planet, and the holiness of Spirit. You love the Holy Spirit. You love the concept of the Holy Spirit. I call on the energy of the Holy Spirit to manifest in the etheric plane. The light of the Shekhinah, the Mother energy, announces her presence as the Holy Spirit. You are holy! *Atah Kadosh, Ruach Ha Kodesh*—Spirit of Holiness. Hearing these words, you understand them. Acknowledge the Holy Spirit within you. Make your spirit holy. It is holy. It is already sacred.

Unification and the codes contained in the Sacred Triangle are going to bring a new level of healing to Earth. It must be a new energy, for the old energy is not sufficient anymore. You want new energy. You want new light. You want holy light and sacred light. Let holy light come to you. It is the holy light that is the foundation for the whole third dimension. The whole third dimension comes from a ray of light.

Conceive of our Father/Mother as a person with his/her eye open. If the eye were to close, then the dimension would evaporate. This is an interesting analogy, because light comes from the eyes. The light emanating from the Father/Mother energy comes from the eyes. Allow your eyes to radiate light even if they are closed. Radiate light. You are creators of light too! You are creating the light for the Sacred Triangle.

First comes light, and this light is the basis for this dimension. If you follow the strands of this light, it goes back to the moment of the big bang. Your astronomers are looking for the first light; it is fascinating. We can go in the etheric to the moment of the first light. We acknowledge light as the foundation for the third dimension. It is true that light can become corrupted here. It is true that there is darkness here and that light has been misinterpreted. A pure light has come here, but there has been confusion and misunderstanding. You are holy beings. Bring together light. Clarify the factors leading to the necessity of unification. I love the beauty of the Sacred Triangle. I love the acknowledgment of the ascended natives, and I love your openness to the Arcturians.

THE *KABALLAH*

Nabur and Archangel Metatron

There are many things from the *Kaballah* that would be helpful to integrate now. The *Kaballah* is basically a galactic energy that has been brought to Earth. The central core of *Kaballah* deals with the Zohar energy. The Zohar energy is the infinite light that comes from the Creator Source and is manifested in this galaxy and our universe. The Creator Source has deemed such a light source to appear and he/she communicates through this light. Those of higher power can interpret and receive messages from this light. How fantastic it is to relate to the Zohar light and step down the energy so that this light becomes interpretable to those of lower vibrations.

How is it that you can relate to this communication? Receiving the light is communicating with it. This is a communication beyond words. In your highest meditative state, you are not in the ego, or the verbal, state. If you attempt to verbalize what you are experiencing, the verbalization can often cause the energy to be stepped down.

I want to bring you this experience of the Zohar light. It is my belief that you are ready to experience that light. You are ready to have the experience without any thoughts or any interference from attempting to verbally explain or categorize it. The ego also includes the ability to think, using the categories and the duality that is so prevalent in this culture. Your culture is not really geared up for fifth-dimensional work. The Arcturians and others of higher light have a culture based on fifth-dimensional being. Their cultures make room for nonego and nonverbal experiences. In the Arcturian ships, for example, you will find places where beings can go to be in tune with this light.

THE LIGHT OF SPLENDOR

Unification with this light will benefit you by raising your vibration. Raising your vibration will bring you to another level so that you can experience the Zohar light more directly. To experience the Zohar light fully, you must go beyond the realm of nothing or "no thing." Incidentally, the light is increasingly becoming stronger as you are getting closer to the ascension. You are getting closer to being able to use Jacob's Ladder. The Ladder is going to be here. You have heard of merkava travel. *Merkava* is the Hebrew word for chariot. When the ancients did astral traveling, they would use the image of the chariot. I know that you do not have chariots in your culture; you have automobiles, and some may use the etheric automobile as their merkava vehicle. Some of you may use etheric pyramids. In Jacob's Ladder, we have the concept of climbing up to the fifth dimension by using an etheric ladder. This ladder is as effective a tool as the merkava chariot.

Remember, you are a vessel. The word *Kaballah* means "to receive." The problem with being a vessel is that you must be strong enough to receive the currents coming down. You are now becoming strong vessels, and you are going to be able to hold more light. We are going to go into the level of strongly receiving the Zohar light. *Zohar* is the Hebrew word for splendor, or brilliant splendor. Sananda receives this light directly, and then he steps it down so that you can access it more easily.

Atah Gebur, Atah Gebur, Atah Gebur Adonai. Atah Gebur Adonai. Atah Gebur Adonai. You are great, *Adonai.* I call on the light from the highest source, the light from the Creator, *Elohim Adonai.* I move up to the divine light, the holy light, *Aur Ha Kodesh.* Let this holy light come down. *Aur Ha Kodesh.* Holy light! I now move up to the infinite holy light: *Aur Ain Sof*—the light that has no end. *Aur Ain Sof. Aur Ha Ain Sof.* We move up now to the Infinite One without end.

Now we go from this *Ain Sof,* to the Central Sun energy in the galaxy. This is the source of the Creator energy in this galaxy—the Central Sun. Go in your mind to the Central Sun. Traveling to the Central Sun is going to the core of this galaxy. All galaxies are linked together through the central sun of each galaxy. Each central-sun galaxy is linked to the primordial Central Sun—the primordial center. As you go to the primordial center, you will then come to the primordial man—the primordial Adam.

When the universe was created, the light formulated the primordial man, Adam Ha Kadmon—the primordial Adam. All of the souls on Earth originated through his mind. His mind is directly linked to the Creator mind. We will go now inside the body of Adam Ha Kadmon. [Chants.] When you are in the body of Adam Ha Kadmon, then you are also connected to the Central Sun of the Milky Way. You are connected to all of the central suns of all of the galaxies in the universe as well as to the Creator Light.

I want you to look outward through his eyes. The eyes of Adam Ha Kadmon can see the infinite light of the *Zohar* that is manifested. Look through his eyes and see that light going infinitely through the entire universe. It is a brilliant, infinite light that is through the whole universe. That infinite light is circling around the universe and through every being. Know that this light is reaching you and going into your vessel and physical body. You are now tuned into the vibration of the Zohar light. You are connected! You can receive. All beings that are alive have the codes to receive this infinite light from the Creator. You have taken the right path. Take this light and follow it to different areas.

RECEIVE THE LIGHT

I want you to take the light and connect to the Arcturian stargate. Travel in your mind to the Arcturian stargate. Above the stargate, you will see a huge crystal. This is a special crystal that is designed to receive and magnify this light. We are talking now about fifth-dimensional beings and fifth-dimensional energy that is designed to receive and magnify the light from the *Zohar*, this brilliant light—the Light of Splendor. Stay connected to the eyes of the Adam Kadmon; his eyes are gleaming. I want you to now put the image of his eyes into your eyes, even though your eyes remain closed. You can picture the image of his eyes looking at the Zohar light and receive it into your eyes. Now you can see this wonderful light.

You can use this light to connect with an entry into the fifth dimension. Those who see the splendor of the Lord, *Adonai Elohim, Adonai Echad*, will be granted entrance into the gardens and into the world to come, *Olam Ha bah*—the fifth-dimensional realm of the City of Justice. You need only see and feel this light to gain access to this entry point.

Your Arcturian friends can appear to you. You will see that their eyes are especially adapted to seeing this wonderful Zohar light. They can use their beings and whole bodies to receive and process light. As you move up to the higher dimensions, you become totally devoted to this task of experiencing this beautiful Zohar light, and your higher self can connect and work with this light. The higher self is going to connect totally to your lightbody. Your lightbody is always receiving the vibration from the light of the *Zohar*.

I call on Sananda to intensify the light now so that we can build up to a higher intensity of Zohar light. Look at the light through your eyes that are closed. Open your interior eye and your third eye. There is a pathway for all to follow who wish to come to a higher place. The evolution of your souls involves moving to a place, to a realm, where you can be more in alignment with this wonderful light.

You will take the higher aspects of self with you when you leave Earth. You have higher, middle, and lower self. The work that you are doing now to connect to the higher self will help you to enter the fifth dimension more easily. See and hear the Zohar light now. We can go to multidimensions. See and hear. Everything has a tone and a visual presence. Sananda is an intermediary. See light coming down to you from his eyes, heart, and hands. He is assisting you, helping you to step down this brilliant light.

The Tree of Life, *Etz ha Chayim*, is a way of describing how the energy is stepped up and stepped down. You are stepping up energy. You are stepping up your receptors. Think: "Holy light, holy light." With your mind and eyes, look at the Arcturian stargate. As you are looking at the Arcturian stargate, our dear friend, Archangel Metatron wishes to speak with you.

✳   ✳   ✳

THE BEAUTY OF LIGHT TRAVEL

My friends, this is Metatron. *Kadosh, Kadosh, Kadosh Adonai Tzevaoth!* Holy, holy, holy is the Lord of Hosts! You are coming to such a high level that we are able to assist you in unlocking any codes that are limiting you so that you can participate fully in the light experience that is before you. Special compensation and special grace is before you now so that you can have this wonderful light experience. Unite the energies that you have been working on. You are being granted this ability to be on a higher light frequency. Hear my words and let them step up your light intensity, your light frequency, and your ability to receive. Holy, holy, holy, *Kadosh, Kadosh, Kadosh Adonai Tzevaoth, Adonai Tzevaoth*. Holy, holy, holy is the Lord of Hosts. *Neshamah*—higher lightbody. You are light!

Look through the eyes of Adam Ha Kadmon. Look for infinite light and the beauty of infinite light and of holy light. You can look and see the infinite light that goes on forever. Come down this tunnel that is before us by the stargate. Come into this tunnel of light with me. We will go on a journey of light travel, down the corridor with your mind and with me and all this Light! We are traveling so fast through this light corridor. *Atah Gebur Adonai, Atah Gebur Adonai, Atah Gebur, Atah Gebur.* This is Hebrew for "You are great, *Adonai*; You are great, *Adonai.*"

We look down the tunnel. The tunnel is infinite. It is a special strand of light that is more intense than what we had seen before, yet you can tolerate it. Follow the light. It is infinite; it comes from a point of origin that is infinite. It is the Infinite Mind of *Elohim* that is manifested in this way. We cannot describe it; we cannot even speak of it. Come into the Source of this light, which is the Mind of Elohim, the Source of all light. Blessed are you, O Lord our God, King of the Universe forever and ever. [The Hebrew translation of forever is: *Le-olam Vaed.*]

May the codes in your lightbody be forever bound by this wonderful opening that we experience together. There are many angels around this tunnel. Now you must connect this light source to your lightbody, which is still partially attached to your physical body. Send down this light into your physical body back on Earth. Let it come in through your crown chakra and fill your physical body.

Now I call on you to return from the tunnel, passing through the Arcturian stargate on the outer edge and back into the physical body. You are now filled with this new energy. You can look out as your eyes are closed and see infinite light. You are now connectors on Earth to this infinite light, this holy light—*Aur Ha Kodesh.* You are now holy spirits on Earth. You now walk as holy lightbeings. Light is streaming from your eyes, from your hands, from your crown chakra, from your third eye, from your heart chakra, and from your feet. You are all filled with light energy, and you have a strand of Zohar light with you. This is Metatron.

CHAPTER 22

ON ACCELERATING YOUR ACTIVATION

Ashtar[1]

I am Commander Ashtar from the Space Command, working with the White Brotherhood.[2] Greetings to all who may be listening to or reading this transmission. There are many new souls who are coming into consciousness at this point. These new souls are experiencing an awakening that usually occurs among old souls who have had many incarnations or who are preparing to enter their final life patterns before ascending. Now we are entering a state in which there are many new souls who have not incarnated as often.

Many of you have the conception that an old soul is superior to a new soul or is wiser and able to move into higher realms of understanding. Although there is some truth to that, you must now realize that new souls have a special adaptability that will help them become open to newer energies. Likewise, older souls sometimes become stuck in certain patterns and must incarnate often to learn lessons. What I am telling you is that there are many new souls on your planet who are awakening and that this is an exciting development. They are activating just as you might have activated several years ago.

UNLOCKING GENETIC CODES

One of the major problems, from your perspective, is that when there are plateaus and periods of limited access to higher energy, you will enter a stage in which you do not feel entirely in resonance. In these cases, it is best to adhere to some type of structure such as a minor ritual or a daily meditation.

Regarding the ascension process, you must understand that it is coming in waves. At times, there are pulsations that are deeper and have more intense energy bursts than usual. In order for the maximum benefit to occur, as many souls as possible will need to experience awakening and acceptance of the path of ascension.

Being on the path of ascension and ascending are one and the same. Even when you are on the path of ascension, there could be an intervening variable, perhaps due to death, that could prevent you from being in the first wave.[3] The fact that you are on the path of ascension is as important as your actual ascension, for you are then moving in that direction. You have triggered within you deeper avenues toward unlocking genetic codes.

Let me say something about unlocking genetic codes. Many want to know how to do this. First, the codes were placed in people as part of the earlier Adam Kadmon blueprint, which occurred with the prototype of Adam. This code was brought to the Earth plane and inscribed with the help of extraterrestrial "kings" from the planets of the Pleiadians. Other extraterrestrial sources also participated—beings who would be considered part of the high council in our galaxy.

The Adam Kadmon prototype was initialized through your evolutionary development. It was deemed that the species you are a part of would use this code for unfolding. Even though you are not always aware of the codes, the codes are within you. Even your own genetic structure is acting without your awareness. Your cells are changing, you are losing hair, you are gaining weight, you are changing your heart rhythms, and you are breathing at different rates. All this is being monitored through your genetic codes. The Adam Kadmon codes are unfolding even as we speak.

ASCENSION ACTIVATION

How do you become more aware of these codes, and how do you accelerate their action so that you can be at the optimum level? It is important for you to understand that your unfolding has a timetable. It occurs in a certain time frame and with a certain rhythm. Because of the relative shortness of the time now due to the activation, the ascension, and the Earth changes, there needs to be an acceleration of the unlocking so that you can process the codes.

We can focus energy into your genetic structure that will help you to accelerate the unfolding, but it can be done only with your permission. We have to be careful that there is an agreement on your spiritual side to interact with us for the acceleration to occur. Your higher self must be in agreement.

Many want to accelerate, but their higher selves are not in alignment. Your higher self might want you to accomplish certain tasks before it gives permission for acceleration. To properly unlock these codes, you must first give assurance that your soul is prepared for activation. You must say that you will accept the activation, then your genetic structure will unfold at a more rapid rate. Secondly, you must seek to align with an energy such as mine or with the energy from other guides who can help you to accelerate the genetic codes. I will send you energy when I understand you want your genetic codes to be accelerated.

As we send the energy, accept that your genetic structure is being accelerated. A piercing blue light will enter through your crown chakra and begin an activation. It has a center strand of white light. If you hear the Hebrew word *Eh'yeh*,[4] visualize an actual opening and an activation energy. When you use this energy, you are preparing to receive an energy that will accelerate the unlocking of your codes. As you activate, you will gain higher consciousness and draw higher energy to yourselves.

I suggest that in your meditations, you focus on the blue light with the white center coming into your crown chakra. This will activate and accelerate the codes that are placed in all of your chakras. Very simply, you are opening up your chakras by unlocking the codes. You are making the chakra wider, more sensitive, and more receptive. This increase in receptivity will enable you to experience guides from the higher dimensions. You will experience this in body, spirit, and mind.

You must focus the energy for a period of time to accelerate your activation. You cannot accomplish it in one experience. A general acceleration has been granted; however, for you to increase your own receptivity, you will have to interface with an acceleration energy beyond the general energy granted to all at this time.

Unlocking genetic codes will positively accelerate karma, remove karma, and disconnect you from karma. Karma will not stick to you! This is a good way to perceive the process, and it is important for us as well. We are not incarnating or manifesting. To interact with you, we are required to pass special vibratory tests to ensure that we will not incur karma.

The starships are able to send accelerated energy to you. Part of the original plan of the starseeds was that they were to interact with the starships to help unlock codes and to accelerate energy fields. Were you to be in a "beaming-up" situation, then you would experience an activation. When you give us permission, we will guide you toward acceleration.

Notes:

1. Ashtar is the commander over a group of spiritual beings dedicated to helping Earth evolve. The beings Ashtar commands exist primarily in the fifth dimension and are very committed to serving Earth. They come from many parts of the universe, and many of these beings have experienced life on Earth or in the Pleiades. For more information, see Dorothy Roeder, *Reach for Us* (Flagstaff, AZ: Light Technology Publishing, 1991), 164.
2. The White Brotherhood is a spiritual hierarchy of ascended masters residing in the fifth dimension. White is not used here as a racist term. It refers to the white light or higher frequency that these masters have attained.
3. It has been said that there will be three waves, or major uplifts, for the ascension. Each will occur at a different time.
4. The supreme name of God. In Hebrew, *Eh'yeh* is the first person singular form of the word meaning "to be" or "I Am." This is the new name for God given to Moses in Genesis 3:14. The divine presence is called by three names: *Elohim*, *YHVH*, and *Eh'yeh*. Only *Eh'yeh* was new to Moses.

CHAPTER 23

ASCENSION AND THE
TREE OF LIFE

Nabur

Greetings, I am Nabur. We want to discuss the Tree of Life and its accessibility and expansion. In this time that you are living in, I can assure you that the Tree of Life is more accessible than it has been during any other period on the planet Earth. The original downloading of the Tree of Life was given and expressed through a select few higher beings. Now the information and the blueprint for the Tree of Life and what it represents are being transmitted throughout the planet. This is a positive development.

The original Tree of Life and its expansion represents a galactic spiritual knowledge that was given throughout the galaxy and the universe. This is the reason why it is so special, because it represents the multidimensional nature of reality and manifestation.

UNDERSTANDING THE TREE OF LIFE

The Tree of Life demonstrates the existence of other dimensions. It starts with the idea that manifestation on Earth is at the bottom part of the tree, but Earth can only manifest through work done in the higher spheres or higher dimensions. This means that the reality of Earth and the third dimension is based on work that is occurring in other spheres and in other dimensions. What you experience on Earth is only an aspect of your multidimensional nature, and what you see on Earth is only one aspect of the many different interactive and dimensional forces that are occurring. These forces have led to the manifestation of the third dimension and Earth.

The first obvious understanding of the Tree of Life has to do with duality. The tree has three columns. The nature of the tree has to do with the essence of the right and the left columns and how a balance can be found through the middle column, as well as with the top and the bottom energy of the columns. The top, which is known as *Kether*, or the crown, represents undifferentiated, unmanifested light that comes from the Creator. It is the driving force, but it is undifferentiated. Undifferentiated energy means that it is not useable and not comprehendible in a human's mind.

This undifferentiated energy follows a downward path to manifestation. On the path to manifestation, the undifferentiated energy must go through dualities: It must go through the right and the left columns and eventually into the center. The center represents the balance. In order for manifestation to occur on the multidimensional higher spheres, balance and harmony occur in the upper levels. This means that for humankind, there is a possible energy of perfect balance, even though that energy of perfect balance may be in the higher sphere, or higher realm. You can therefore understand that there is a higher balance despite the polarities, despite the conflicts that you see now on this planet.

The second understanding of the Tree of Life has to do with the nature of the Tree itself, as well as the nature of the ten spheres. These are all dynamic spheres, dynamic energy fields that are representative of the creation and the process of creation. Therefore, our knowledge of this process is increasing as humankind is expanding its consciousness. What was unknowable about the Tree of Life in AD 1400 is now more knowable. There is new information, knowledge, and ability for humanity to understand. That is why we say that this Tree of Life is more accessible than ever to humankind. The tree represents how both consciousness and beings are manifested.

Most importantly, this is a dynamic Tree of Life, which means that there is a changing aspect to each element. Humankind could not have known this undifferentiated energy 600 years ago. Now humankind has a higher ability, a higher energy, and a higher awareness through which it can comprehend the undifferentiated energy. I am not saying that humanity can totally grasp undifferentiated energy, but there is a new understanding of the Tree of Life to be grasped. The crown, for example, can also be understood from the integrations of the Tao into the Tree of Life. The new ideas that are now available have to do with the unities that are now occurring in some religious thinking and with some religious mystical unities. New mystical insights offer humanity a greater ability to comprehend the Tree of Life and undifferentiated energy. Modern people can comprehend the forces and harmony that can exist to balance polarities.

THE PERFECTION OF GOD

Another insight into the Tree of Life is that the bottom influences the top as much as the top influences the bottom. That is a confusing issue to some people, because many would say that only the higher energies influence the manifested Earth. How is it possible that the manifested Earth can influence the higher spheres?

The new understanding of the Tree of Life is going to show that not only does the energy come down from the top through all the spheres and manifest, but there is also a backflow of energy. This backflow has to do with the nature of climbing, or ascending, the Tree of Life. This is very similar to climbing Jacob's Ladder. The Tree of Life is going to bring people closer to the concepts of ascension because, essentially, ascension is using your higher energy to climb the Tree of Life into higher spheres and multidimensionality.

There are safeguards so that a total collapse, or a total destruction, on the third dimension would not harm the higher realms, yet the higher realms are interactive with the lower realms. In order for that interaction to occur, there must be an interdimensional exchange. This concept that I describe leads to the conclusion that *Kether*, the higher crown, is affected by what is going on in the lower realms. This seems to be in contradiction to the idea that God is perfect, because being perfect, God would not be affected by what is going on in the world. Yet this overlooks a key point— any characteristic or any feature that humankind can have or manifest is also a feature of the Godhead energy. In other words, God can also have that trait, which means that God is affected by what is going on in the lower realms by people. It is a characteristic of God, so God is affected, but this does not diminish God's perfection. This is the paradox.

In order for the truth of *Kaballah* to be manifested, an integration of all higher consciousness with the third dimension must occur. One must understand the nature of this interaction of the higher and lower realms. The truth is that God is a personal God as well as an undifferentiated energy beyond the comprehension of humankind. People have the ability to be affected by higher and lower energies. That is a characteristic that would be included in God's energy field as well. The contradiction is that God is still in a state of perfection even though affected by his creation.

Why should God not be affected by his creation? That is why God sends messengers. That is why God sends angels. That is why God sends emissaries such as Sananda to Earth to foster unity that will effect a higher evolution. This means that the nature of the Tree of Life is an expression of how one gets closer to God. One doesn't directly interact with God; one must follow a pattern of energetic emanations. This is what the Tree of Life represents.

HIGHER ENERGY

It may be helpful to discuss balancing mercy versus judgment as another aspect that is represented on the two pillars on the Tree of Life. It is well known that there were worlds before this world in which mercy reigned. But mercy was so out of balance that devastation resulted from too much kindness. Therefore, kindness is now being counterbalanced by judgment, but judgment can also be too strong. This new balance is now being manifested in the world.

You know that too much understanding and too much kindness will allow certain groups who have evil intentions to gain control of resources and planetary ideals. They may have evil intentions; therefore, one of the lessons now on the planet has to do with understanding the nature of kindness or mercy versus judgment. This lesson is going to be manifested in many other aspects in terms of how people are going to deal with Earth and Earth changes.

Hidden knowledge, which is known in Hebrew as *D'aat*, is now going to be manifested because it no longer needs to be a hidden sphere. A new sphere, the sphere of manifestation between the third and the fifth energy, is being downloaded into the Tree of Life to accommodate the energy for ascension. This new sphere is directly above *Malchut*, or the Kingdom.

We want to point out that while the Tree of Life is the core of the *Kaballah*, it is not the sole aspect of the *Kaballah*. There are many related theories and ideas that form the basis of the *Kaballah* and, in particular, relate *Kaballah* to the energy of modern-day ascension. The first concept and energy in *Kaballah* relating to ascension is reincarnation. It is well known by many Kaballist masters, teachers, and rabbis that this life is not our only life. You have had multiple lives. In fact, many of the Kaballist rabbis, including the *Baal Shem Tov*, were able to read and see your past lives by looking either at your hands and reading palms or by looking at your foreheads. The basic idea of reincarnation relates to the concept that, in order to ascend, you must be able to complete your life lessons and your soul lessons.

In the *Kaballah*, ascension was offered to several Biblical figures. The raising of the chariots by Elijah and also the ascending of the etheric ladder by Jacob are two examples. These were examples of how the people were able to transcend the concept of waking consciousness and go to the higher realms. Most impressive and most important in all of the Biblical and ancient histories is the ascension of Enoch. "Enoch walked with God; then he was no more, because God took him away" [Genesis 5:24, New International Version]. This means that Enoch ascended, transformed, and became Metatron. The point is that in order to ascend, you have to be of a higher energy. Enoch was already of a higher energy, as were Eliahyu and Elijah. Elijah used the energy of the *merkava*, or the etheric energy of the chariots, to ascend.

THE UNIFICATION OF THE REALMS

The *Kaballah* also offers the directions for completing soul lessons. The diagram, or the blueprint, for completing the soul lessons is offered in the Tree of Life, where there are twenty-two paths. Those twenty-two paths are often correlated to the major arcana in the Tarot cards. These paths are based on the concept of duality and integration of duality, which is one of the key lessons in the *Kaballah*. In the ascension, one needs the ability to integrate and unify duality. A key concept in the *Kaballah* is the work of unifying the upper and lower realms. One talks about unifying the energy on the third dimension with the higher energy as a way to raise the sparks and raise lower energies. When we talk about ascension, we talk first about raising the third-dimensional energy to the energy of the fifth dimension.

Kaballistic interpretations of the traditional stories in the Old Testament also reveal the existence of the other dimensions. In these interpretations, the Garden of Eden is actually a description of the fifth dimension. The fall of Adam and Eve from the Garden is, in fact, a metaphor for leaving the fifth-dimensional realm, leaving the realm for unity to the realm of duality in the third dimension. It is in the duality of the third dimension that the energies must be reunified.

Unlocking the codes of ascension is another important Kaballistic concept for the ascension. The key concept here is that higher consciousness needs to be unlocked. Normal consciousness needs to be transcended so that one can perceive the higher realms. The perceptions of the higher realms enable one to ascend: You have to have a preconceived notion that there are other realms. Not only that, you have to practice going to these other realms. These higher realms are often referred to in the Hebrew lessons of *Kaballah* as the *Olam Habah*, or the world to come. The world to come is really the fifth-dimensional world. It is not the astral world but the higher world to come.

Using the sacred codes to unlock the energies of ascension means that you are to unlock your perceptual field, your perceptual awareness, so that you can perceive and direct your ascension. This is the key: You perceive and direct your ascension. You notice that in Jacob's Ladder, Jacob sees the ladder going upward. Enoch experienced a higher energy, and he immediately disappeared from Earth and ascended. Enoch represents the ascension in total; in the ascension you seem to disappear from Earth but actually transform into your fifth-dimensional self.

You can unlock the codes of ascension using the sacred words: Holy, holy, holy is the Lord of Hosts. This also demonstrates a key Kaballistic idea for the ascension. This key concept is the power of the Hebrew sound and the power of the word. In this case, *Kadosh, Kadosh, Kadosh, Adonai Tzevaoth*, chanted with intention and the right enunciation of power, opens the inner sanctuary in the mind to unlock the keys of ascension. This will then allow the ascension to occur. Again, you must unlock the codes of ascension for yourselves to ascend, and the key is speaking these sacred words or sounds. One of the basic concepts of the *Kaballah* is that sound has healing power and energy.

In the modern ascension, a sound will be enunciated at the start. This sound will be heard by those who are the starseeds and higher beings. That sound will also unlock the codes of ascension and signify the beginning of the ascension. Remember, there will be a sound that you will hear at the ascension. You can unlock your personal codes of ascension through sounds and sacred words, but the ascension energy itself will occur and be announced through a sacred sound that has not yet been emitted. It may be similar to the sound of the *Shofar* (Hebrew for Ram's horn).

THE SPHERE OF *TIFERETH*

The Tree of Life is holographic. By holographic, I mean that there are trees within trees. One aspect of one sphere has all ten spheres in it, and then you ascend in that sphere so that you can go up to another sphere. The concept I want to introduce now is the center of the Tree. After you cross the center sphere, which is called the sphere of the *Tifereth*, you can touch all other spheres. This center is a sphere of harmony that has often been referred to as the sphere of Sananda. One goes up the ladder, so to speak, so that one can ascend.

After transcending the center sphere, the sphere of *Tifereth*, you then reach a point where you no longer need to return to the third dimension. You do not need to reincarnate back on Earth. In other words, in modern-day ascension and in ascending the Tree of Life, you reach a point at which you do not have to return to Earth, because you have reached the higher-dimensional world.

This is another key concept in the *Kaballah*: There are other higher-dimensional worlds. Therefore, you can reach a higher plane. Once you reach higher planes, there is no need to return to the lower world, which is the third dimension. The *Kaballah* offers a powerful tool for self-work. That tool of self-work means that working the spheres helps you to understand and complete the lessons of this incarnation. When the lessons are completed, then you are able to ascend. I know that you may not complete all lessons 100 percent in this lifetime, and so we have the concept of grace. Grace originates in the *Kaballah*. It originates in the sphere of kindness, or mercy. There is mercy when the soul offers you grace so that you can take advantage of this opportunity for ascension.

Kaballah means to receive, and this beautiful message of the Tree of Life needs to be received and processed. The energies of the *Kaballah* point to the Tree of Life as a blueprint not only for personal ascension but also for planetary ascension. These concepts contained in the spheres are also keys for planetary work. There are codes and instructions within the Tree of Life through which the planet and the interaction of the planet with higher beings can be activated for a planetary ascension.

✻   ✻   ✻

In the *Kaballah*, the master of ascension, the key leader of ascension, is Archangel Metatron. Enoch is the first recorded higher being who was able to ascend. He became Metatron, and Metatron is overseeing the ascension for many people. The angelic world is cooperating and working to assist all of you in ascension.

Archangel Michael is also involved in the ascension and, of course, is a great Kaballistic leader and teacher. Your cords of attachment can be cut with the assistance of Archangel Michael. It is hard for all of you, no matter how much energy work you do, to eventually release yourselves from the Earth world alone, so call on the angelic presence. Call on Archangel Michael and Archangel Metatron, and they will assist you on all levels for your ascension. I am Nabur.

CHAPTER 24

THE TREE OF LIFE: COMPASSION AND JUDGMENT

Archangel Michael

The lecture opens with three high, clear resonating tones of a bell, and then Shaloooom *is intoned by David and echoed by the congregation:* "Shaloooom. Shaloooom."

Greetings, I am Archangel Michael. We will continue our discussion of the Tree of Life, because the Tree of Life is the diagram that offers you certain methods to raise your vibration. This is a method that has been used for centuries, but it also represents a diagram that comes from galactic sources.

There are several important points to be understood about the Tree of Life as a tool for your ascension. I will use the example of the opposites as expressed as loving kindness on one side and judgment on the other. We know that this is not the first world that the Creator has made. There were other worlds that failed. Juliano has already hinted to you that there are planets that are in the same position as Earth—or were in the same position in the past—and those planets did not survive.

In the Tree of Life and in the way of thinking of the *Kaballah*, if the world has too much kindness and too much understanding, then the world can also be in danger. One example for too much compassion that I like to use is this: We understand that this world has problems with violence and terrorism. If you were able to capture a terrorist, then you might say, "I understand. I have compassion for you. I understand your feelings." But if you let him go, he might do the same thing again—he would repeat the violence.

So there are situations in which too much compassion and too much understanding does not help. You can understand that if there were only understanding and compassion in the whole world, then that version of the world would be out of balance and would not function well, and it would eventually destroy itself. So the fact is that compassion must be counterbalanced by judgment, but the judgment itself must be given with strength.

SOMETIMES PAIN DOES NOT YIELD GAIN

One favorite story in the *Kaballah* is that of King Solomon, who exemplified the characteristic of judgment. Now, I will not repeat the whole story, but you might know that two women claimed to be the mother of the same child, and no one could figure out who was telling the truth. So as a judge, King Solomon said, "Fine, I will cut the baby in half, and I will give half to you and half to you." When one of the women stepped forward and said, "No, no, give it to her. I do not want my baby harmed," Solomon knew immediately that this was the true mother of the child, and he gave the child to her.

Now, this is a very good story; it illustrates that sometimes the judge must be harsh. You may ask, "Would the judge have actually cut the baby in half?" The answer is, no, he would probably not have. But with judgment, comes responsibility and strength. This means that judgment counterbalances compassion, so you need judgment to make the world work.

But there are also worlds in which judgment is too harsh, and those worlds suffer and can be destroyed as well. I can tell you that there have been some cultures—in Afghanistan for example—in which the people in control were too harsh and used judgment too strongly. And when judgment is passed too strongly, then that world also can be destroyed. So this tells you that judgment must also be balanced with compassion. This is the rule in the worlds that exist throughout the galaxy.

You and I together can look at Earth and ask, "Is there too much judgment? Is there too much compassion?" These questions yield very complicated and difficult answers. But we must look at this with honesty. If people are destroying Earth, then compassion is not going to help. Listen to how crazy this could sound: "Oh, I understand that you want to make a lot of money; I know that you need to be a millionaire. You can take all of the oil you want out of the earth. Oh, I'm sorry that you destroyed this part of the ocean, but I understand." Now that's not a good position to take. In the *Kaballah*, there is a saying that compassion is not necessary when what the person is doing is bad. But then there is also judgment, and in order to be the judge, you must have strength.

This is the problem: Who has the strength to be the judge when someone is doing something that is this bad? Now, people might respond, "Only God can be the judge; it is not our role to be the judge." But it is your role to be protectors. The *Kaballah* and the Tree of Life say you have both traits, but it must be done in a balanced way. This is why the Torah was given to the people; this is why the Ten Utterances, the Ten Commandments, were given. It was to teach that there must be some judgment, that there are some things that have to be judged. This is part of living in the third dimension.

You can see that there have been planets that had only strong judgment, and those planets did not survive. Many of you here have been to Atlantis, and some of you suffered. You knew that the people in power were creating energy experiments that were going to destroy their world. What were you to do? You saw that it got out of control, and it was very painful to see the end. You do not want to see that end again here. So I will tell you this: You have to be true to yourself. If there is an action that you need to take, you must look within yourself.

Now you have the diagram of the planetary Tree of Life. Many of you are taking action by participating in the crystals and in spiritual work for Earth, but there are some of you who might decide to take other steps. I will not suggest what they should be, but both you and I know that there are many people on Earth who are very dense. They will look at your spiritual work and the work of ascension and laugh. That is their right, because Earth is a free-will zone. But they do not have the right to destroy this planet. So you can decide what other actions you can take with other people. This is a calling.

Your calling may be to educate others about what is going on; your calling might be to help a child—a child who is a Violet child, a child who is of the Indigo. You may need to somehow support a stronger environment. So your path as a lightworker can include other work that is based on your judgment, and there are people who are going to be involved in judgments. Juliano has told you that you already see that some of the institutions responsible for controlling parts of your life are acting like criminals. Their actions have created a great deal of suffering. As we get closer to 2012, their criminality is coming to the surface, and people are saying, "Oh, we trusted those people to handle our children; we trusted those people to educate us. Now we see that they were acting like criminals." Compassion is not called for in this situation, and we must stop this. Sometimes you have to be the judge or support those who have the strength to be the judge.

FIFTH-DIMENSIONAL PRINCIPLES OF A JUST SOCIETY

I want to explain this part of the 2012 energy field. There is a change in the institutional structure of society. The Tree of Life shows that the energies of both judgment and compassion are also manifested in another sphere below. The other sphere below has to do with the planetary Tree of Life and with the creation of a just society based on fifth-dimensional principles. This sphere, this *Sephiroth*, is going to gain more energy and more awareness. Having a balance of judgment and compassion is going to create a necessity for a more just society based on fifth-dimensional principles. So let's think about what this society would be like.

You know that in the fifth dimension and on fifth-dimensional planets the basic society is not founded on the principles of wealth and greed, but rather it is based on the higher, fifth-dimensional principles of cooperation, sharing, and the distribution of wealth. It is based on a more spiritual way, not on a way of controlling people. We know the history of this idea, and some people have taken the idea that I have just expressed and changed it to make it sound like it was something else. But new ideas about how to set up a society are coming into the consciousness of everyone who is a lightworker.

There are going to be new ways of thinking that have not been discussed before. There are going to be new ideas about how to set up a political world, how to set up a world sociologically, and how to deal with religious thinking. This was one of the most beautiful contributions of the Arcturians to the new world view, to the new world thinking that is called the Sacred Triangle.

Juliano taught people this idea. There is an aspect of all religions that is interrelated, an aspect you may call "unity thinking," or unity consciousness. So every religion, as it started and got into its mystical energy, shares this wonderful unity view. You as lightworkers know this as the White Brotherhood and the White Sisterhood. We do not use the word "white" to mean skin color but rather as the symbol of purity. We say, "Protect me with the white light; bring down the white light to me." This is one aspect of the new unity thinking.

The other aspect that Juliano shares is this: "Let's honor the Native American people of the planet, because they understand the importance of forming a relationship to Gaia, to the spirit of Earth. They understand that we must do this. It is not a question of *should* we do it; it is something we *must* do." Juliano calls this biorelativity. More importantly, you must understand that societies in this galaxy who do not form this relationship with their planet perish. Now that is harsh judgment, isn't it? But we know through our contacts with the space brotherhood and sisterhood that there have been other planets that have self-destructed. So we want to have a new consciousness based on Earth as a spiritual being. We see that this has happened with the Native Americans already. You already have the basic thought patterns and the basic system in an existing structure within them.

GALACTIC SPIRITUALITY

As we look at galactic spirituality, we see that the archangels are involved in the fifth dimension. The basic core of *Kaballah* is to understand the nature of this reality and the nature of God. You can understand the nature of God by understanding the nature of his creation. The creation is beautiful because this is a world and a universe with multiple dimensions. This is a universe in which there are higher extraterrestrial beings. This is a universe in which souls like you get to graduate into higher realms.

Galactic spirituality says, "Look, there are other dimensions. Look, there are other planets. Look, there are other higher beings, and you are not alone on Earth." Isn't it a good idea to learn about their experiences? Isn't it a good idea to hear and contact the ascended masters, the higher-dimensional beings? And yes, you can graduate too—you can get away from the duality and go to a higher dimension. This whole area of thought is called galactic spirituality. Juliano has asked that we teach the integration of all three of these concepts.

Now, because you are all reaching toward the higher dimension known as the fifth dimension, you can bring down energy from that higher level. This energy can be undifferentiated energy, but it also can be differentiated energy. This means that you can bring down specific energy. Maybe you are a doctor doing scientific research and you want to discover a cure for AIDS or tuberculosis. This is a very concrete subject. You might ask, "What does this have to do with the fifth dimension?" Yet the fifth dimension can help you because it helps to get you out of the box and gives you a new perspective.

I can tell you that Albert Einstein was in the fifth dimension with his work. Everyone knows that he was a starseed, even though he would not admit it. Many physics professors now understand the new reality. This idea of bringing down fifth-dimensional energy, of course, could also apply to politics, religion, and economics, as well as to the management of the environment. But it is revolutionary; it will totally change how your society on Earth operates.

What all of the prophecies have said is that 2012 is going to be a time of change. You all agree that change is necessary, but to change all of these systems in such a short time would create a total upheaval. So how is this to happen? Will you just see the destruction of the systems? You almost saw the destruction of the financial systems in 2008. It recovered, but the problem was not really solved. What I am suggesting is that there are economists who are starseeds and that they are able to connect and bring down new ideas to solve this problem.

Each of you has a soul mission in the view of *Kaballah*, and throughout all of these workshops, people have asked, "What am I supposed to do? Why am I here?" Everyone has a different soul mission. Your soul mission may be within your family: Maybe you have a son who has fantastic energy and is brilliant, and you need to make sure that he is developed properly. Maybe he is going to make some major contribution to all of the problems we just talked about. Some of you might have specific professions that you might not consider important. But I can tell you that if you are an economist or you're doing some kind of money management, it may be very important to work from a higher prospective. I do not have time to go into all of the different professions, but I think that you get the idea.

THE *KABALLAH* CAN HELP YOU TO MANIFEST YOUR DESTINY

I want to switch to the idea of the personal Tree of Life, because we have said that this Tree of Life can be used as a way of creating a paradigm for the healing of the planet. I gave you one example of balancing judgment with compassion. I also explained that those two in balance would create a new structure based on a new system of greater light. But let us look at your own personal development, because you have a personal evolution that is going on right now. You may have emotional problems, such as depression or anxiety, or maybe you have relationship problems and you are here to learn personal lessons.

For example, some of you—especially women—have had previous lifetimes in which you were very much controlled. You were not allowed to have spiritual freedom, and some of you may actually have been punished for expressing spiritual views and spiritual energy. So when you think about the ascension, think about it in terms of the planetary energy I have talked about, but also remember to think about it in terms of your personal evolution and the personal lessons you need to go through.

I will briefly use the paradigm of compassion with judgment to explain this process. Here the Tree of Life is a little bit different than from the planetary level. But at the same time, it is very similar, so we jovially say "similar but different." It is good to have compassion for yourself, but we know that sometimes people themselves are their own greatest enemies. We know that many people are very judgmental of the self: "You are not good enough. You didn't do that right. You don't deserve this." Now, this is judgment. Remember when I talked about the planet and I said that if there is too much high judgment, the planet will be destroyed? If you are too judgmental of yourself, if you are too harsh on yourself, then you can destroy yourself as well.

Some of you may have thoughts of judgment against the self; you think that you are not worthy enough to ascend. This is harsh judgment against the self, so we must work in the *Kaballah*. As a tool for ascension, the Tree of Life can help by teaching you that harsh judgment toward yourself must be balanced with compassion. So you need to say and act differently if you are too judgmental. Then when you get that part of yourself in balance, you will be able to manifest your destiny.

The *Kaballah* teaches that each of you has a destiny toward the planet. Now this aspect of the *Kaballah* is new, because in the old *Kaballah*, they did not talk about the planet. In the galactic *Kaballah*, we talk about your mission to the planet, and we also talk about the mission of service: From this, you have the mission of what you are supposed to be learning as a person. For example, this mission has to do with why you might be born in Spain as opposed to India. So there are many specific aspects in your mission of what is called your *Mossel*, your destiny.

BRING DOWN THE HIGHER LIGHT TO THE THIRD DIMENSION

What you need to understand is that the *Kaballah* as the Tree of Life represents energy spheres that must be balanced and activated. This enables you to bring down the highest possible energy into the third dimension so that you can manifest, act on, and bring down this higher light. We call the base the third dimension. In Hebrew it is called *Malkuth*, which means the "kingdom."

May you have the energy and the power to activate all aspects of the Tree of Life within you. Then you can completely fulfill your soul purpose and bring down that energy into the Earth. We will end this lecture by singing a word with which you are very familiar and that also has a very high spiritual vibration. As soon as you hear the word, you will recognize it. I will sing it once, I will sing it twice, and the third time, we will sing it together. This will mark the end of our time together for now. It will make everything that I have said go into the deepest parts of you so that you can learn whatever you needed to learn from these words immediately.

[Sings alone.] *Ahh-men. Ahh-men.*

[Sings together.] *Ahh-men.*

I am Archangel Michael. Good day.

GLOSSARY

2012 ALIGNMENT

A time when Earth comes into alignment with the center of the Milky Way galaxy. This is also referred to in the Mayan calendar, and prophecies were made for this date. The Maya believed that Earth will come into alignment with the center of the galaxy on December 21, 2012. Some have interpreted the Mayan statements as marking the end of the world. Others say that this alignment represents the transformation of the world. One view is that our world will be born again on December 21, 2012. In *Maya Cosmogenesis 2012*, John Major Jenkins interpreted the Mayan vision of this alignment in 2012 as a union of the Cosmic Mother, or the Milky Way, with the Father, represented as the December solstice sun.

2012 CORRIDOR

A tunnel or corridor to the future time of 2012 when Earth's transformation will be at its height. By projecting positive energy and images into this time, one can help maximize positive outcomes for this time.

ADAM KADMON

The Hebrew term for the primordial or first man. It is the prototype for the first being to emerge after the beginning of creation.

ADONAI

Hebrew name for God, translated as "my Lord."

ADONAI TZEVA'OTH
Hebrew for "Lord of Hosts."

ADON OLAM
Hebrew for "Lord of the Universe."

AIN SOF
In *Kaballah*, the term *Ain Sof* means "that without end." It is sometimes compared to the great Tao. *Ain Sof* is the absolute perfection in which there are no distinctions and no differentiations. It does not reveal itself in a way that makes knowledge of its nature possible.

AMIDAH
A famous Hebrew prayer recited silently during daily prayers.

ARCHANGEL
The term applies generally to all angels above the grade of angel. It also designates the highest rank of angels in the celestial hierarchy. The *Kaballah* cites ten archangels. They are considered messengers bearing divine decrees.

ASCENSION
A point of transformation reached through the integration of the physical, emotional, mental, and spiritual selves. The unification of the bodies allows one to transcend the limits of the third dimension and move into a higher realm. It has been compared to what is called "the Rapture" in some denominations of Christian theology. It has also been defined as a spiritual acceleration of consciousness, which allows the soul to return to the higher realms and thus is freed from the cycle of karma and rebirth.

ASHTAR
The commander over a group of spiritual beings who are dedicated to helping the Earth ascend. The beings Ashtar oversees exist primarily in the fifth dimension and come from many different extraterrestrial civilizations.

ASTRAL PLANE
The non-physical level of reality considered to be where most humans go when they die.

ATAH

The Hebrew word for "you." It is used in prayer to refer to the Creator.

ATAH GIBUR ADONAI

Hebrew for "You are great, Adonai!"

AUR

The Hebrew word for "light." It is also spelled *Or.*

AUR HA KODESH

Hebrew for the "holy light."

AUR HA MOSHIACH

Hebrew for the "light of the Messiah."

BARUCH

The Hebrew word for "blessed," often used in referring to the Creator.

BARUCH HU

The Hebrew transliteration for "Blessed are You," referring to the Creator.

B'NAI ELOHIM

The children of light. The Hebrew words for the "sons, or brotherhood, of the Elohim."

CHAKRAS

Energy centers of the human body system. These centers provide the integration and transfer of energy between the spiritual, mental, emotional, and biological systems of the human body.

CHASHMAL

A mysterious Hebrew term mentioned in Ezekiel's vision. It refers to the mental state through which one passes when one ascends from the level of speaking to one of pure mental silence and sensitivity.

EH'YEH ASHER EH'YEH

In Hebrew, the name of God given to Moses at the burning bush in Genesis 3:14. *Ehiyeh Asher Ehiyeh* is the full name translated as "I shall be that I shall be" (also translated "I am that I am"). In Hebrew, this is also known as the supreme name of God. The correct Hebrew translation is "I will be that I will be."

Elohim
In Hebrew, the name that describes the Creator in chapter one of Genesis.

Etz-ha-Chayim
Hebrew for "Tree of Life."

Gadol
The Hebrew word for "great." It is also used as an adjective when describing God.

Gurhan
A spiritual entity from the Andromeda Galaxy in the seventh dimension.

Hu
The Hebrew word for "he." In prayers it can refer to the Creator.

Ibbur
The Hebrew word describing the entry of another soul into a man.

Kaballah
The major branch of Jewish mysticism. The Hebrew word *Kaballah* is translated as "to receive."

Kadosh
Hebrew word for "holy."

Kadosh, Kadosh, Kadosh Adonai Tzevaoth
Hebrew for "Holy, holy, holy is the Lord of Hosts." This is a powerful expression that, when toned, can raise one's level of consciousness to new heights and assist in unlocking the codes for our transformation into the fifth dimension.

K'dushah
A Hebrew prayer, translated as "Holiness."

LIGHTBODY
The higher etheric spirit body that is connected to the highest soul energy.

MAGGIDIM
Hebrew word for divine spirits speaking to a Kaballist.

MEEK
The Hebrew word for "king." It is used in prayer to refer to God.

MERKAVA
In Hebrew, this term means "chariot," and in modern spirituality, it refers to a chariot in etheric form that is used to bring spiritual seekers to the higher dimensions. Also spelled *merkaba* and *merkabah*. In *Kaballah* it is the term that means God's throne-chariot, referring to the chariot of Ezekiel's vision. It is also used in describing a branch in *Kaballah* called "merkava mysticism."

METATRON
Tradition associates Metatron with Enoch, who "walked with God" (Gen. 5:22) and who ascended to heaven and was changed from a human being into an angel. His name has been defined as the Angel of Presence, or as the one who occupies the throne next to the divine throne. Another interpretation of his name is based on the Latin word *metator*, which means a guide or measurer. In the world of the Jewish mystic, Metatron came to hold the highest rank among angels. According to the Arcturians, Metatron is associated with the stargate and is assisting souls in ascension to higher worlds.

METATRONA-SHEKHINAH
These are two names for the divine presence. It is that aspect of the Goddess energy that is present on Earth.

MICHAEL
This being's name is actually a question that means, "Who is like God?" He is perhaps the best known of the archangels and is acknowledged by all three Western sacred traditions. He has been called the Prince of Light, fighting a war against the sons of darkness. In this role, he is depicted most often as winged, with unsheathed sword—the warrior of God and slayer of the dragon. His role in the ascension is focused on helping us to cut the cords of attachment to the Earth plane, which will allow us to

move up to higher consciousness. In the *Kaballah* he is regarded as the forerunner of the Shekhinah, the divine Mother.

MONAD
The original, elemental creative force.

NABUR
A Kaballistic rabbi and teacher of the author in a former lifetime.

NEFESH
The Hebrew word for "animal soul," or "lower soul," representing the entire range of instincts. *Nefesh* is the raw vital energy needed to live on this planet.

NESHAMAH
Hebrew word for the spiritual portion of the soul, or higher self. It is the intuitive power that connects humankind with the Creator, the highest of the three parts of the soul that transcends third-dimensional reality and Earth ego to link directly to the divine light.

QUAN YIN
A female member of the Spiritual Hierarchy. In her previous Asian incarnation, she performed many acts of kindness and compassion and is known as the Goddess of Mercy.

RABBI HAYYIM VITAL
A Kaballist rabbi who lived from 1543 to 1620 in Safed, Palestine.

RAPHAEL
Raphael is perhaps the most endearing of all the angels—and the one most often depicted in Western art. His name means "God Has Healed." His career seems to focus on medical missions and he helps people to heal human maladies. He was the angel sent by God to cure Jacob of the injury to his thigh when Jacob wrestled with his dark adversary. He is also considered to be the guardian of the Tree of Life in the Garden of Eden.

RUACH HA KODESH
The Hebrew words used to describe the state of enlightenment, literally translated as the "Holy Spirit."

SANANDA

Sananda is the one who is known to us as Master Jesus. He is considered one of the greatest Kaballists of all times. His galactic name, Sananda, represents an evolved and galactic picture of who he is in his entirety. In the *Kaballah*, Sananda is known as Joshua ben Miriam of Nazareth, which translates as Joshua, son of Mary of Nazareth.

SHABBAT

Shabbat is the Jewish Sabbath, on Friday. Kaballists believe that the Shekhinah comes on *Shabbat* to be with man and to help make that day holy.

SHEKHINAH

In Hebrew, "the divine Mother." *Shekhinah* is the frequently used Talmudic term denoting the visible and audible manifestation of God's presence on Earth. In its ultimate concept, it stands for an independent feminine entity, the divine Mother.

STARGATE

A multidimensional portal into other higher realms. The Arcturian stargate is very close to the Arcturus star system, and it is overseen by the Arcturians. This powerful passage point requires that Earthlings who wish to pass through it must complete all lessons and Earth incarnations associated with the third-dimensional experience. It serves as a gateway to the fifth dimension. New soul assignments are given there, and souls can then be sent to many different higher realms throughout the galaxy and universe.

STARSEEDS

Earth beings throughout our current modern age who have previous lifetimes in other parts of our galaxy. They also have a great awareness that there are other beings living in our galaxy and in the universe.

TIKKUN

In Hebrew, this term means "restoration," or "the divine restoration of the cosmos." In *Kaballah*, this refers to the concept that the vessel holding the light from the Creator was broken and that it is the task of humans to help restore it.

TREE OF LIFE

The Tree of Life is a galactic blueprint for the creation of this reality. It includes ten energy codes placed in spheres in the shape of a tree. These codes are used for individual and planetary healing. The three spiritualities of the Sacred Triangle are included in the Tree of Life. The Tree of Life is not flat, but multi-dimensional and holographic. The Tree of Life has pathways for manifestation found in its twenty-two lines. The Tree of Life connects to the energy of the cosmos. [See the separate Tree of Life section later in this appendix.]

VYWAMUS

A fifth-dimensional soul psychologist known for his insight into the psychology of Earth problems and the resolution of issues related to starseeds incarnated on Earth.

WHITE BROTHERHOOD

The White Brotherhood is a spiritual hierarchy of ascended masters residing in the fifth dimension. White is not used here as a racial term. It refers to the white light, or higher frequency, that these masters have attained.

YIHUDIM

The Hebrew word for "unifications." Kaballists believe that humans help to unify the two aspects of the Godhead through prayer. It is important to enunciate a simple statement prior to reciting a prayer to the effect that one's intention is to bring about the unification of God and the *Shekhinah*.

ZADDIQ

Hebrew word for "wise man."

ZELEM

Hebrew for "man's ethereal body," which serves as an intermediary between his material body and his soul.

ZOHAR

The Book of Splendor: a thirteenth-century Spanish mystic's guide to Kaballism.

NOTES ON HEBREW PRONUNCIATION

This is not intended to be a comprehensive pronunciation guide to Hebrew—modern or ancient, classical or rabbinical. Like most languages, Hebrew has undergone many regional and temporal changes in its structure and pronunciation.

The primary purpose of this guide is to assist the reader in producing verbal sounds that resonate with their respective energies. A full survey of all possible sounds expressible in the Hebrew language is beyond the scope of this book.

Most of the consonantal sounds are very close to how they have been rendered in this text. There are a few sounds which will be unfamiliar to those who do not speak Hebrew. These sounds are listed below.

q: used instead of "k" to indicate a similar sound, but further back on the palate, with the lips more rounded

ẓ: a sound quite close to "ts," as in English "its," with the "t" sound perhaps less stressed

ch: guttural, as in German "Bach"

sh: as in English "she"

r: not quite equivalent to the English "r," instead much more like the "r" in French—further back on the palate and rolled forward

Note on doubled consonants *kk, dd, bb,* and so on. These must be pronounced fully, but smoothly. So *zaddiq* is "zad-diq" and *tikkun* is "tik-kun," with no noticeable pause between the doubled consonants, but each is pronounced.

For vowels, the following pronunciation is given as a guide. There are few more disputed topics in the study of ancient languages than the pronunciation of the vowels, especially in a living ancient language like Hebrew, which has historically been written with no vowels.

A: as in "father"
E: approximately between "eh" and "ay"
I: as in "ink"
O: as in "over"
U: approximately between "under" and "super," but tending toward the long sound
AI: like "eye"
AU: approximately between "auger" and "aura"
AH: usually at the end of a word, it has a similar sound to the "a" by itself, like "a" as in "father," but lengthened and slightly aspirated—think just like English "ah"

NOTES ON THE TREE OF LIFE

The Tree of Life (Hebrew: *Etz ha Chayim*) is mentioned sparingly in this text, but as it may be unfamiliar to some readers, a diagram and brief explanation follows. There are many other sources of information on the Tree of Life and its cosmology, and readers are directed to those sources in the event that they take an interest in this concept.

The Tree of Life is a cosmological map, or framework, for creation, used by Kaballists to aid in understanding the relationships of all things in the universe. It consists of the ten *Sephiroth* (spheres) connected by twenty-two paths, and it represents a kind of framework for describing the hierarchy of existence, from the limitless light of *ain soph aur* all the way down to the base stuff of creation.

The first three *sephiroth* are the supernal triad. These form the level sometimes collectively referred to as the *neshemah*, the highest level of the soul, ascended consciousness, and self.

• *Kether* is the *sephira* closest to God. This is *sephira* is the aspiration of the Gnostics, seeking union with the divine. The name means "crown."

• *Chokmah* is the prime movement in existence, the initial spark. The name itself means "wisdom."

- *Binah* is primordial duality, that which receives and is acted upon by the forces from *Chokmah*. The name means "understanding."

The next six *sephiroth* are the part of creation sometimes referred to as the ruach, containing the powers of intellect and consciousness.

- *Chesed* is the loving grace of God, the requisite energy to sustain creation. The name means "mercy."

- *Geburah* is the strength to endure, the power of judgment, and the will of intent. The name means "severity."

- *Tiphareth* is the Christ consciousness, the balanced compassion expressed as the equilibrium between *Chesed* and *Geburah*. The name means "beauty."

- *Netzach* is initiative, strength of will, and overcoming. The name means "victory."

- *Hod* is faith, surrender, and letting go. The name means "glory."

- *Yesod* is remembrance, subconscious connection, and ethereal awareness. The name means "foundation."

Below *Yesod* is the level reffered to as the *nefesh*, containing the physical realm, lusts and passions, and the animal soul:

- *Malkuth* is the realization, creation, the material. The name means "kingdom."

These are but brief and very incomplete descriptions, and the reader is encouraged to undertake further study. The *sephiroth* all have many different qualities, and the paths that connect them can be powerful tools to the spiritual aspirant.

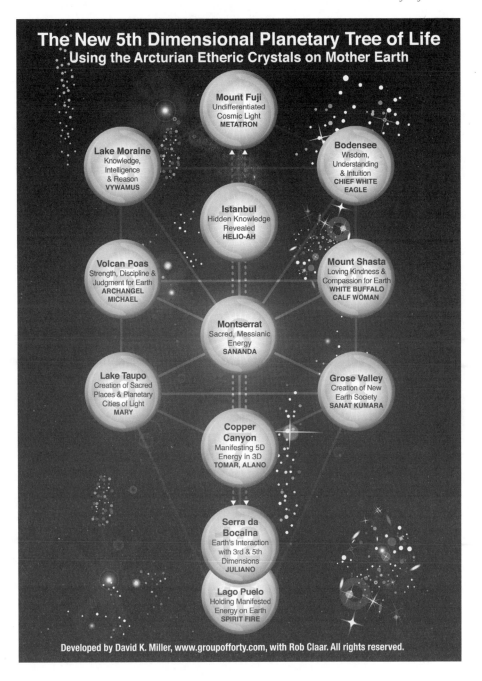

The New 5th Dimensional Planetary Tree of Life
Using the Arcturian Etheric Crystals on Mother Earth

Mount Fuji
Undifferentiated
Cosmic Light
METATRON

Lake Moraine
Knowledge,
Intelligence
& Reason
VYWAMUS

Bodensee
Wisdom,
Understanding
& Intuition
CHIEF WHITE
EAGLE

Istanbul
Hidden Knowledge
Revealed
HELIO-AH

Volcan Poas
Strength, Discipline &
Judgment for Earth
ARCHANGEL
MICHAEL

Mount Shasta
Loving Kindness &
Compassion for Earth
WHITE BUFFALO
CALF WOMAN

Montserrat
Sacred, Messianic
Energy
SANANDA

Lake Taupo
Creation of Sacred
Places & Planetary
Cities of Light
MARY

Grose Valley
Creation of New
Earth Society
SANAT KUMARA

Copper
Canyon
Manifesting 5D
Energy in 3D
TOMAR, ALANO

Serra da
Bocaina
Earth's Interaction
with 3rd & 5th
Dimensions
JULIANO

Lago Puelo
Holding Manifested
Energy on Earth
SPIRIT FIRE

ABOUT THE AUTHOR

David K. Miller's original spiritual study was the *Kabbalah* and Jewish Mysticism. He began trance channeling his Kaballistic guide and teacher, Nabur, on a camping trip at Sublime Point on the North Rim of the Grand Canyon in 1991. His focus in channeling includes ascension and integrating Jewish mysticism with soul development. He channels more than fifteen guides, including the Arcturians, Sananda, Mary, Ashtar, Archangel Michael, and Nabur, a Kaballistic rabbi.

David has published five books and over fifty articles in both American and Australian magazines. He currently does phone readings and conducts workshops focusing on the concepts and techniques of ascension, healings, and psycho-spiritual issues while also working full time as a medical social worker. David resides with his wife Gudrun in Prescott, Arizona.

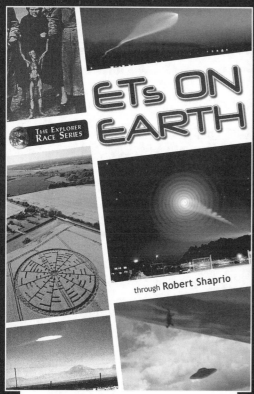

PLANT SOULS SPEAK
A NEW WAY OF INTERACTING WITH PLANTS

THROUGH ROBERT SHAPIRO

"What we intend to speak about—if I may speak in general for all plants—is how you can interact with plants in a more benevolent way for you as the human species. For a long time, you have been clear on medicinal uses of leaves and stems and seeds and flower petals and so on, but you are only getting about one-tenth of the energy available to you that way. It is always better to interact with the plant and its energies in its live form, but you need to know how.

"The intention of this book is to reveal that formula so that you can stop searching, as a human race, for the magical cures to diseases by exhausting the supply of life forms around you, when a much simpler process is available. This book will not just comment on things you know about but show you what you are missing in your interaction with plants."

—Dandelion

$16.⁹⁵

ISBN 978-1-891824-74-6
Softcover, 286 pp.

Chapters Include:

Cherry Tree	Maple Tree	Palm Tree	Peach Tree
Pine Tree	Redwood	Walnut Tree	Brown Rice
Crabgrass	Oat Grass	Wetland Grass	Angelica
Bamboo	Corn	Daffodil	Dandelion
Hibiscus	Holly	Ivy	Kelp
Marijuana	Orchid	Rose	Sage
Soy Bean	White Rose		

TIME AND THE
TRANSITION TO NATURAL TIME

THE EXPLORER RACE

TIME

AND THE **Transition to Natural Time**

THROUGH ROBERT SHAPIRO

$16.⁹⁵

ISBN 978-1-891824-74-6
Softcover, 286 pp.

"The purpose of this book is to provide a context for your lives in the sequence you find yourselves in now. This explanation of time—and, to a degree, its variables—is being provided for you so that you will understand more about your true, natural, native personalities and so that you will be reminded that you are, as you know, in a school and that this school is purely temporary.

You don't come here very often to this place of linear time; like your own human lives, you are in school for only so long, and then you live your lives. When you exist beyond this school, you will find all those lives infinitely easier, and even as the Creator, your lives will be easier than they are in their single, linear lives that you're living now, because you will have all your components."

—Founder of Time

Chapters Include:

Time Is Now Available for Your Personal Flexibility

You Live in a Stream Hosted by Planet Earth

Moving Toward Complete Safety and Benevolence

The Gift of Time

You Are Here to Learn About Your Personal Physicality

Letting Go of Conflict in the Next Focus

Your Blinders Are Coming Off

Time Is an Application for Expansion

Transition to the Future in Warmth and Safety

Linking from Future Selves

Making the Transition through Deep Sleep

There Are Many Expressions of Time

Shamanic Secrets Mastery Series

Speaks of Many Truths and Reveals the Mysteries through Robert Shapiro

Shamanic Secrets for Material Mastery

This book explores the heart and soul connection between humans and Mother Earth. Through that intimacy, miracles of healing and expanded awareness can flourish. To heal the planet and be healed as well, we can lovingly extend our energy selves out to the mountains and rivers and intimately bond with the Earth. Gestures and vision can activate our hearts to return us to a healthy, caring relationship with the land we live on. The character of some of Earth's most powerful features is explored and understood, with exercises given to connect us with those places. As we project our love and healing energy there, we help the Earth to heal from human destruction of the planet and its atmosphere. Dozens of photographs, maps and drawings assist the process in twenty-five chapters, which cover the Earth's more critical locations.

498 p. $19.95 ISBN 978-1-891824-12-8

Shamanic Secrets for Physical Mastery

Learn to understand the sacred nature of your own physical body and some of the magnificent gifts it offers you. When you work with your physical body in these new ways, you will discover not only its sacredness, but how it is compatible with Mother Earth, the animals, the plants, even the nearby planets, all of which you now recognize as being sacred in nature. It is important to feel the value of oneself physically before one can have any lasting physical impact on the world. If a physical energy does not feel good about itself, it will usually be resolved; other physical or spiritual energies will dissolve it because it is unnatural. The better you feel about your physical self when you do the work in the previous book as well as this one and the one to follow, the greater and more lasting will be the benevolent effect on your life, on the lives of those around you and ultimately on your planet and universe.

576 p. $25.00 ISBN 978-1-891824-29-5

Shamanic Secrets for Spiritual Mastery

Spiritual mastery encompasses many different means to assimilate and be assimilated by the wisdom, feelings, flow, warmth, function and application of all beings in your world that you will actually contact in some way. A lot of spiritual mastery has been covered in different bits and pieces throughout all the books we've done. My approach to spiritual mastery, though, will be as grounded as possible in things that people on Earth can use—but it won't include the broad spectrum of spiritual mastery, like levitation and invisibility. I'm trying to teach you things that you can actually use and benefit from. My life is basically going to represent your needs, and it gets out the secrets that have been held back in a storylike fashion, so that it is more interesting."

—Speaks of Many Truths through Robert Shapiro

768 p. $29.95 ISBN 978-1-891824-58-6

Phone: 928-526-1345 or 1-800-450-0985 • Fax: 923-714-1132